As a former school principal, church senior pastor and Bible College campus leader, I have had the privilege of working alongside many outstanding educators and thinkers. Sharon Kohring is at the head of that group. Sharon combines a lifetime of faithful study, pastoral ministry, deep reflection, Spirit-soaked insight and Bible teaching, together with real-world living, to build a rich tapestry of understanding the character of God. She has a delightful and effective way of weaving Biblical exposition and personal anecdote that brings truth to life.

Murray Averill
Executive Director, Alpha Australia

Any book that starts by wanting to disciple others in order to help them understand the Lord better and then goes on to refer to A_____ and J.I. Packer has my attention. And that's exactly what Sharon Kohring has done in Oh My God - Let Me Tell You About Him. In a warm, relatable style she takes us on an adventure toward understanding and grappling with some of the most misunderstood attributes of God, breathing hope and life into our walk with Jesus. Beautifully written, pastoral in nature, and rich in insight - this book will become a useful tool to anyone who wants to know God better. And in a world that is in a current state of turmoil, reflecting again on the unchanging nature and character of God has perhaps never been more vital for humanity.

Cass Langton
Global Worship and Creative Pastor, Hillsong Church

Do you remember your favourite teacher back in your school days? I do! Just the mention of the name brings to remembrance a person who treated me right, made me feel safe and worthy of investing into, but also had the uncanny ability to bring clarity and understanding to an inquisitive mind. Sharon Kohring is one such teacher! She has a gift, taking crucially important truths and unpacking them into understandable, enlightening principles that can now make sense and are useful for life itself. This book handles the most important of matters – knowing God

– revealing who He is based upon decades of personal revelation and in-depth, thoughtful Bible investigation. In an increasingly shaky world of flimsy life foundations and confusion as to the essence of God, I can recommend this book to anyone and everyone who has an inquisitive mind and an open heart.

Steve Dixon
State Pastor for Queensland and Northern Territory,
Hillsong Church Australia

Sharon is an obvious lover of God's Word, a genuine lover of people and has a unique ability to help individuals apply truth to their lives. Having worked together whilst we lived in Brisbane, we've always loved her insights that spring from a beautiful, contagious relationship with God. We've seen, first hand, her ability to trust God in challenging seasons whilst continuing to steadfastly help others. We are convinced that this book will be a game changer for you as you discover more of God's nature. Our world needs this rock-solid assurance now more than ever!

Steve and Rachel Mawston
Elders and Senior Leaders, Soul Church UK

Being a life-long, passionate student of God's Word, in this must-read book, Sharon Kohring explores the many facets of God's unchanging character. It is truly beautifully written with richness found in God's Word, personal reflections, tasteful illustrations and vulnerable experiences in her journey of intimacy with Jesus. In a world where there is so much uncertainty and change, Sharon masterfully points us to God's unshakable and unchanging nature. No matter where you are in your own journey of faith, this book will stir up your passion to know Him more. Sharon has been a personal blessing to us and an inspiration in the way she gently guides, encourages and develops young leaders within our church family.

James and Elida Turner
Campus Pastors for the Gold Coast,
Hillsong Church Australia

If you have ever had questions about the attributes of God or you are in a place where you want to know more about God, this book is for you. Sharon Kohring has written a delightful piece that illuminates the characteristics of God, drawing from everyday experiences with which we all can relate. As you take a journey through this book, not only will you learn so much about how good and great God is, but your life will be transformed by knowing how much God loves you. A must-read.

Dr. Rita Okoroafor
Author, *Morning Does Come*, Nigeria

In this book, Sharon Kohring shows her deep love of God as she takes you on a wonderful journey by sharing her insights in an informed and practical manner. Sharon's love of God's Word and her desire for others to love Him and His Word are inspiring, refreshing, and very evident. Sharon is a passionate teacher who has made her classroom accessible to us all. This book is a timely reminder of the characteristics of God.

Margaret Aghajanian
National Pastoral Care Oversight, Hillsong Church Australia

Having known Sharon for 30+ years and being involved with her in a variety of ministry opportunities, I can vouch for her deep spiritual walk and excellence in all areas. Written in a very readable style, Sharon's book brings theology and the attributes of God into a very accessible format well-suited to this generation. Her application questions and activities at the end of each chapter make the content very concrete and practical. This book will provide an invaluable and desperately-needed resource for enabling people to connect right theology (attributes of God) to a healthy life and fruitful ministry.

Dr. George Schultz
Learning Center Director, Center for Intercultural Training, USA

A journey through the
characteristics of God

Oh My GOD!

Let Me Tell You About Him

Sharon Kohring

Oh My GOD! Let Me Tell You About Him
Copyright © 2021 by Sharon Kohring

Cover and interior design: Stuart Smith
Photography: RAW by Nature Photography

All rights reserved. No part of this publication may be reproduced, stored in a retrieval system, or transmitted in any form by any means, electronic, mechanical, photocopy, recording, or otherwise, without the prior permission of the author.

Unless otherwise indicated, all are from the New International Version, NIV. THE HOLY BIBLE, NEW INTERNATIONAL VERSION®, NIV® Copyright © 1973, 1978, 1984, 2011 by Biblica, Inc.® Used by permission. All rights reserved worldwide.

Scripture quotations marked ESV are taken from the ESV® Bible (The Holy Bible, English Standard Version®), copyright © 2001 by Crossway, a publishing ministry of Good News Publishers. Used by permission. All rights reserved.

Scripture quotations marked MSG are taken from **THE MESSAGE**, copyright © 1993, 2002, 2018 by Eugene H. Peterson. Used by permission of NavPress. All rights reserved. Represented by Tyndale House Publishers, Inc.

Scripture quotations marked NKJV are taken from the New King James Version®. Copyright © 1982 by Thomas Nelson. Used by permission. All rights reserved.

Scripture quotations marked NASB are taken from the NEW AMERICAN STANDARD BIBLE(R), Copyright (C) 1960, 1962,1963,1968,1971,1972,1973,1975,1977,1995 by The Lockman Foundation. Used by permission.

Scripture quotations marked AMPCE are taken from the Amplified Bible (AMPCE), Copyright © 1954, 1958, 1962, 1964, 1965, 1987 by The Lockman Foundation. Used by permission.

Excerpts taken from *God Came Near* by Max Lucado. Copyright © 1986, 2004 by Max Lucado. Used by permission of Thomas Nelson. www.thomasnelson.com

Excerpts taken from *The Jesus I Never Knew* by Philip Yancey. Copyright © 1995, 2002 by Philip Yancey. Used by permission of Thomas Nelson. www.thomasnelson.com

Excerpt(s) from *Generous Justice: How God's Grace Makes Us Just* by Timothy Keller, copyright © 2010 by Timothy Keller. Used by permission of Dutton, an imprint of Penguin Publishing Group, a division of Penguin Random House LLC. All rights reserved. Copyright © 2018 by Timothy Keller. Used by permission of Hodder & Stoughton Limited, London.

Excerpts taken from *One Thousand Gifts* by Ann Voskamp, Copyright © 2011, 2021 by Ann Voskamp. Used by permission of Thomas Nelson. www.thomasnelson.com

Excerpts taken from *The Grace Awakening* by Charles Swindoll, Copyright © 1990, 1996, 2003 by Charles Swindoll. Used by permission of Thomas Nelson. www.thomasnelson.com

Excerpts taken from *God and the Pandemic* by N.T. Wright, Copyright © 2020 by N.T. Wright. Used by permission of Zondervan. www.zondervan.com

Excerpts taken from *Determined to Believe? The Sovereignty of God, Freedom, Faith, and Human Responsibility* by John C. Lennox, © 2017 by John C. Lennox. Used by permission of Zondervan. www.zondervan.com

Excerpts taken from *The Knowledge of the Holy* by A.W. Tozer Copyright © 1961 by Aiden Wilson Tozer. Used by permission of HarperCollins Publishers.

First printing 2022
Cataloguing – in – Publication data available

ISBN 9781922411327 (International Trade Paperback)
ISBN 9781922411334 (eBook)

With a heart full of love for my dear grands, the next generation of Kingdom influencers:

Jayla, Sage, Ivy, Hunter, Lily, Banjo, Rayden, Ella

...tell to the coming generation
the glorious deeds of the Lord, and his might,
and the wonders that he has done.

Psalm 78:4b ESV

CONTENTS

Author's Note — X
Introduction — XI

PART ONE: His Goodness — 1

Chapter 1 God is Good — 3
Chapter 2 God is Merciful — 23
Chapter 3 God is Gracious — 39
Chapter 4 God is Compassionate — 57
Chapter 5 God is Patient — 69
Chapter 6 God is Loving — 83
Chapter 7 God is Faithful — 107

PART TWO: His Purity — 127

Chapter 8 God is Holy — 129
Chapter 9 God is Righteous — 145
Chapter 10 God is Just — 157

PART THREE: His Greatness — 173

Chapter 11 God is All-Powerful — 175
Chapter 12 God is All-Knowing and All-Wise — 197
Chapter 13 God is Everywhere-Present — 213
Chapter 14 God is Sovereign — 223
Chapter 15 God is Immutable — 249

Concluding Thoughts — 260
Gratitude — 268
About the Author — 270

AUTHOR'S NOTE

Recently, I was with a group of young leaders in our church for a discussion around some of their questions as disciples of Jesus. It was beautiful to see their commitment to a deeper walk with the Lord. A couple of questions related to basic Bible study – what were helpful tools and helpful approaches? I mentioned that I was taking a break from my regular Bible reading schedule to study the attributes of God. The response from one was, "Oooooh, I'd love to do that. Is there a verse in the Bible that lists them all?"

I would have been delighted to simply give them a chapter and verse. But I was stumped. They could do personal word studies, I'm sure. But how would they know what words to even look up? So, my quick answer was to suggest two classic, much-loved books – one by A.W. Tozer and one by J.I. Packer – which will each be quoted in the following chapters. That's how I had created my list many years ago. The question got me thinking, though… and now, here we are.

This book takes us on a journey through the main characteristics of God. Whether a follower of Jesus or a sceptic of faith, we are all invited into a deeper understanding of God – our God who can be known and can be trusted.

INTRODUCTION

Perhaps you are familiar with the age-old children's prayer:

God is great
God is good
Let us thank him
For our food.
Amen

It might appear to be trite, but it's pretty accurate theology. We acknowledge the truths of who God is and then we respond to that truth with simple gratitude, saying "let us thank him".

Seemingly, most of the attributes of God can be grouped into these two categories: good and great. I have, therefore, ordered the chapters from good to great. The good aspects of God's character are attributes that all of humanity are able to exemplify because we are all made in the image of God, our Creator. Not one of us could ever be good to the level of God's goodness. But, in various ways, it is possible to see the goodness of God in any human. And those who carry the name of Christ-follower, those who are redeemed by the sacrifice of Jesus and filled by the Holy Spirit, are truly able to demonstrate attributes that are good.

On the good-to-great continuum, there are at least three attributes that relate to God's purity. These are transitional; they are both good and great. These attributes are, in many ways, unique to God. However, as we become more Christlike, we are able to begin exhibiting some elements of these characteristics, though never to his level of perfection.

Then there are the GREAT attributes. These are the characteristics of God that involve his transcendence (being above and beyond all else). No matter how loving, patient, and good I might be in any given moment (I was going to say "day", but it couldn't last that long), I will never demonstrate the great attributes that are ascribed only to God. I cannot speak anything into existence. I cannot know tomorrow. My power is incredibly limited.

It's important that we remember, even as we desire to be Christlike in our hearts and actions, that we must adopt this mantra – "You are God and I am not!" A study of the character of God reminds us of that humbling reality.

A word about "magnify"

Oh, magnify the Lord with me, and let us exalt his name together!
Psalm 34:3 ESV

This verse has baffled me. For a very, very long time. My distorted thinking went like this – God's big; I'm small. Why would a little-Sharon want to make the big-God look big? He IS big!

But I had the wrong lens. I needed to think telescope, not microscope.

Each type of scope uses the science of magnification where lenses bend light so that we are better able to see. However, they differ greatly. A microscope makes something small that is close seem bigger than it actually is while a telescope makes something big that is far away seem closer to us and closer to its actual size.

The sun is our closest star. It's not very big compared to other, more distant, stars. Yet those stars seem much smaller than our sun and some of them are actually invisible to our eyes. The problem with our point of view is our inability to see. So, a telescope "gets us closer" as it makes our view of the sun closer to its true size. The reason we are invited to magnify God is not that he is small; it is because we lack perspective and proximity.

The foundation: "eternal"

None of the attributes of God began to exist and none can ever become more than each already is because God is both eternal and immutable. A chapter at the end of the book deals, specifically, with God's immutability (his unchanging nature). It is placed after all of the other attributes to remind us, at that point, that none of the characteristics of God we discussed will change. "Eternal" is a description of God that is foundational to each of his attributes. None of his attributes began or were added; every characteristic of God is eternal so we'll consider that attribute, now, to set our baseline for every chapter.

"Eternal" is one of those words that applies to God while a different word describes humanity. In Psalm 90:2 we see that God always was. "Before the mountains were born or you brought forth the whole world, from everlasting to everlasting you are God." In John 3:16 we see that through Jesus, when we believe in him, we will have everlasting life. "For God so loved the world that he gave his only begotten Son, that whoever believes in him should not perish but have everlasting life" (NKJV). God is from everlasting to everlasting. And for those who put their trust in Jesus as their Saviour, though they are not FROM everlasting, they will be TO everlasting.

When I worked in Kids' Ministry long ago, I taught a series on the attributes of God. There is no better way to clarify your theology than to try to teach it to children! When teaching the eternality of God, I used two large balls of yarn. I asked a child to come to the front of the kid-filled room and stand in a spot that represented "today". He was instructed to hold onto one end of the yarn and roll the ball of yarn behind him. The yarn was rolling into "yesterday". There was still a huge amount of yarn on the ball when the yarn hit the back wall. And that's what happens when we look back in time. We never can get to where it started; there's always more yarn to unroll.

Then, I asked the child who was still standing in "today" to roll the second ball of yarn forward into "tomorrow". As far as that ball could go, there was still more yarn to be unrolled. And that's my fallible illustration of this word – eternal. We cannot get to the beginning of the story of God and we cannot get to the end of his story. He is without beginning and he is without end.

In Psalm 90:2, seen above, we read that God is from everlasting to everlasting. This means that if we start from today and go back to all of the yesterdays, he is forever. And if we start from today and go forward into all of the tomorrows, he is forever. However, in the verse describing the life of those who believe in the gift God gave each of us in Jesus Christ, we see that there is one "everlasting" and it is forward-facing, into our tomorrows. Simply put, "eternal" is without beginning and without end while "everlasting" is used, in general, to mean without end.

How, then, does this relate to all of the other attributes of God? Basically, God did not BECOME anything. He did not grow into any of his attributes. Because he, alone, is eternal – all that he is he has always been and all that he is he always will be. So, God did not become merciful when someone needed mercy. He is mercy. God did not acquire power from somewhere outside of himself when power was needed. God is power. God always was complete and always will be complete. He is eternal.

It's all about "trust"

For sake of an illustration, no matter your marital status, for just a moment imagine that you are not married. Imagine that a stranger came up to you and said, "God told me to marry you and he said we need to marry right away!"

You would say, "Wait just a minute. Who are you? I don't even know your name! I don't know anything about you! I don't know you at all. Why should I even believe that you've heard from God? Why should I trust you in any way?" And that would, most likely, be the end of the conversation. There is no foundation upon which to even begin a conversation so certainly there is no foundation upon which to build a marriage.

Could it be that the reason we struggle with trusting God is because we don't know him very well? Between what we know about him and who he actually is… there is a major gap. How intimately we know him compared with how intimately we could know him… another major gap.

Our ability to trust God increases as our relationship with God grows. And that simple truth is my major motivation for this book.

We each need to know God better so that we each are able to trust him more. So, trust is an individual and personal thing.

For it to last, our trust has to be based on truth. So, trust is a right-thinking thing.

Trust is not sustainable if that trust is only academic. So, trust is a transformational thing.

And it all comes to nothing without intimacy with God. So, trust is a relational thing.

Grant me, Lord, to know and understand which is first,
to call on Thee or to praise Thee? And, again,
to know Thee or to call on Thee? For who can call on Thee,
enot knowing Thee? For he that knoweth Thee not,
may call on Thee as other than Thou art. Or, is it rather,
that we call on Thee that we may know Thee?

Augustine of Hippo[1]

Embrace pondering

Do you remember what I said about how magnifying God helps adjust our perspective and our proximity? Whenever I have struggled

---

[1] St. Augustine, Bishop of Hippo, *The Confessions*, 397 A.D., Public Domain. (Note: Hippo was in modern-day Algeria).

with life, either my life or life around me, my go-to self-counselling method has been to focus on the character of God. My perspective adjusts to become better focused on my Creator and my proximity moves away from the problem, toward my Redeemer.

Therefore, at the end of each chapter, you'll see some questions for reflection. Raise your hand if you've often skipped those things when you're trying to conquer a book. Yup, my hand is up there with yours. But because the point of this book is not to help you pass a test on the facts of who God is, it follows that it would be valuable to consider what difference each characteristic of God makes in our own, personal lives.

Some of the reflection questions will encourage you to engage another person in magnifying God. I am no Hebrew scholar, but I can use some tools and speak with others who understand Biblical Hebrew more than I (like my son Joey, who is a student of Old Testament Hebrew). By doing that, I learned that Psalm 34:3 not only addresses the shared action of magnification with these words – "with me", "us", "together" – but the verbs translated "magnify" and "exalt" are plural verbs in the original language. So, this verse has very little to do with whispering to yourself about God's greatness on the top of a mountain or even loudly saying, beside a quiet stream, "God, you are so good." Yes, our soul needs that on a regular basis. But there is something about the goodness and GREATNESS of God that compels us to tell others of his wonders and to share with others in the praises of Almighty God.

And so, we are about ready to begin our journey. I'm excited. I hope you are, too. Oh, magnify the Lord with me!

PART ONE

His Goodness

1

GOD IS GOOD

*You are good and do good;
teach me your statutes.*

Psalm 119:68 ESV

Quickly! Name your favourite movie or book, one that you would easily tell everyone is really, really good. Have you narrowed it down? I wonder... what causes you to describe a novel or a movie as "good"? From my point of view, I'd say that most epic books and movies focus on a battle. Whether internally or intergalactically, it is a battle between two forces – good and evil. It is a "good movie" when good wins. It's a really good movie if we collectively stand to our feet and cheer when evil is demolished.

Good and its opposite

Allow me to dip into the deep stereotype of "chick flicks" for a moment. The girl falls for the guy who is battling his internal demons. He's trapped by an addiction or he's trapped by his past, and the dilemma is so debilitating that it causes him to be unloved. He is unloved because he is unlovely. The girl (we could think of her as an angel of mercy) is either his saviour or, at the very least, the catalyst for his salvation. The guy is redeemed; evil is destroyed. Good triumphs in just under two hours.

The intergalactic battles of good and evil are rarely resolved in two hours. Generally, these are battles that require sequels. Tiny glimpses of hope keep viewers coming back for more. It's a hope that possibly, just maybe, one of the many plot twists will straighten out and good will finally be triumphant. This isn't just the theme of good movies; this is the theme of humanity. Why? To answer that question, we need to go back to the beginning.

The word "good" is used very early in Scripture, in Genesis 1, in fact. When God created light, he confirmed that it was good. Throughout the creation account we see that God knows what is good for all that he creates and all that he creates is, actually, good. This is especially impactful when we get into chapters 2 and 3 of Genesis.

In Genesis 2:17 we are introduced to the tree of the knowledge of good and evil. In the centre of this perfect garden stood just one tree whose fruit was forbidden. God made the boundary clear as to what was good (everything else in the entire garden) and what was NOT good (one tree). In chapter 3 we see the story reach the climax. The chapter begins with a temptation and it all goes downhill from there. Its ending is definitely NOT good.

We find that the serpent is able to bring doubt into the picture so that Adam and Eve begin to wonder if God truly meant what he said about the consequences of disobedience. At the core, this is doubting God's goodness – God's integrity, God's perfection, God's heart. In verse 5, the serpent injects distrust of God by saying that God knows that when they eat from that tree, they will be like God. They will know good and evil. God must not be good, runs their logic, because God doesn't want them to be like him. Why would God create something and then forbid it? That can't be good.

From the beginning of the creation of time, we have evidence that God has been, and is, good. And all that he does was, and is, good. Yet the tug-of-war with everything opposed to good goes on to this day. This is why we need to be drawn back to the goodness of the heart of God.

I love You Lord
Oh Your mercy never fails me
All my days
I've been held in Your hands
From the moment that I wake up
Until I lay my head
I will sing of the goodness of God
All my life You have been faithful
All my life You have been so, so good
With every breath that I am able
I will sing of the goodness of God

I love Your voice
You have led me through the fire
In darkest nights
You are close like no other

I've known You as a father

I've known You as a friend
I have lived in the goodness of God

Your goodness is running after,
it's running after me
Your goodness is running after,
it's running after me

With my life laid down, I'm surrendered now,
I give You everything
Your goodness is running after, it's running after me[2]

Tracing God's unflawed goodness

It seems fitting to begin our journey with this attribute of God, the goodness of God, because every specific aspect of God's character is fully good. There is nothing in him that is NOT good. This term speaks to God's perfection. He is so very good that there is no flaw to be found in any part of God's nature. He is so very good that he is perfect. No evil can touch him. God's grace is fully good, his mercy is fully good, his patience is fully good.

But what about when we consider that his justice is fully good, his power is fully good? Maybe those thoughts cast a shadow on the idea of God's goodness. We'll get to those attributes in later chapters, but I want to make it clear, now, that God is good. In every way. There is nothing sinister about his power. There is nothing flawed about his justice. God is good. Completely.

---

[2] Jenn Johnson, Ben Fielding, Ed Cash, Brian Johnson, Jason Ingram, *Goodness of God*, © 2018 Fellow Ships Music / So Essential Tunes / Alletrop Music (Admin. by SHOUT! Music Publishing Australia) / Bethel Music Publishing (Admin. by SHOUT! Music Publishing Australia) / SHOUT! Music Publishing Australia. Used by permission.

> *That God is good is taught or implied on every page of the Bible*
> *and must be received as an article of faith as impregnable as the throne of God.*
> *It is a foundation stone for all sound thought about God and is necessary*
> *to moral sanity. To allow that God could be other than good is to deny*
> *the validity of all thought and end in the negation of every moral judgment.*
> *If God is not good, then there can be no distinction between*
> *kindness and cruelty, and heaven can be hell and hell, heaven.*
>
> **A.W. Tozer**[3]

We can trace the goodness of God throughout the Old Testament. Even in Genesis 3, we see, arising out of the curse on the serpent, the mighty promise of a Redeemer.

> *"And I will put enmity between you and the woman,*
> *and between your offspring and hers;*
> *he will crush your head, and you will strike his heel."*
>
> **Genesis 3:15**

Jesus, as the offspring of the woman, is the fulfilment of that promise. Though the prophecy of Satan striking at the heel of Jesus was overwhelmingly fulfilled when Jesus died upon the cross for our sins, the resurrection of Jesus was triumphant. Ultimately, Jesus will have the last word. Satan will be defeated; his head will be permanently crushed.

---

[3] A.W. Tozer, *The Knowledge of the Holy*, Harper & Row, 1961, 1975 edition, p. 88.

> *Not one word of all the good promises that the Lord*
> *had made to the house of Israel had failed; all came to pass.*
> **Joshua 21:45 ESV**

As we progress through the Old Testament, we continue to read that not one of all of the Lord's good promises to Israel failed. Every single promise was fulfilled. Above, we see Joshua reflecting back over God's goodness toward Joshua and toward the nation he led, stating this reality – all of God's promises were good promises and they all came to pass.

> *Oh give thanks to the Lord, for he is good;*
> *for his steadfast love endures forever!*
> **1 Chronicles 16:34 ESV**

In the passage, above, we see one small piece of a larger hymn. David was establishing a new tent in Jerusalem – a place of worship, a place for the ark of the covenant. He was compelled to testify of God's goodness and he asked Asaph to lead in the worship of their good, good God.

Much later, after exile was followed by a return from exile, Ezra led the rebuilding of the temple in Jerusalem. We see the compulsion to worship their good, good God in the following verse.

With praise and thanksgiving they sang to the Lord: "He is good; his love toward Israel endures forever." And all the people gave a great shout of praise to the Lord, because the foundation of the house of the Lord was laid.

Ezra 3:11

Below, are two examples from the prophets. Even as they speak warnings about the current or coming suffering due to the stubborn rebellion of humanity, they still acknowledge the goodness of God.

This is what the Lord says:
"You say about this place, 'It is a desolate waste, without people or animals.' Yet in the towns of Judah and the streets of Jerusalem that are deserted, inhabited by neither people nor animals, there will be heard once more the sounds of joy and gladness, the voices of bride and bridegroom, and the voices of those who bring thank offerings to the house of the Lord, saying, 'Give thanks to the Lord Almighty, for the Lord is good; his love endures forever.' For I will restore the fortunes of the land as they were before," says the Lord.

Jeremiah 33:10-11

The Lord is good, a refuge in times of trouble.
He cares for those who trust in him.

Nahum 1:7

Good, good

In all of the verses we've considered so far, the word translated "good" is the Hebrew word **towb** or a derivative of it. It seems to be used much like we use our English word to describe something or someone as beautiful, pleasant, agreeable. This means that the same word is used to describe a wide range of "goodness" – from a good cup of tea, to a good word, to a good day, to our good God.

Maybe the recent popularity of the song **Good, Good Father**[4] has helped us face the overuse and familiarity of the term "good". That song grabs my heart because it has such simply profound and profoundly simple lyrics. "Good" is completely inadequate. We have to say it twice in order to communicate how amazingly good God truly is! Somehow, our daily overuse of "good" has caused it to lose some of its "good"-ness! Realising that the goodness of God is a perfect goodness helps to set it apart from the rest. A good cup of tea could be good even though it might be better with milk; a good word could be good even though it might be a bit late and we would have benefitted more from it had it come a week earlier; a good day might be good even though it still has some strong gusts of wind. Only our good God has no "even though". He is good completely, through and through. God's goodness is not just pleasant and agreeable; the goodness of God is without flaw, without evil, without impure motives. God's goodness is the absence of any "not-goodness".

---

[4] Tony Brown, Pat Barrett, *Good, Good Father*, Common Hymnal Digital (BMI) Housefires Sounds, 2014.

God cannot become good-er

This is some very GOOD news – God cannot become good-er than he already is. Why is that good news? It speaks freedom into our souls, freedom from the bondage of a "works" mentality! It means that we are free to be followers of Jesus without any pressure to earn any favour from God. Our attempts to be good will not cause him to move toward us more than he already has. Our prayers will not cause him to turn his face toward us more than it already is.

God cannot become more good because he is always fully good. And he cannot become less good because he is always fully good. Do you feel the freedom in this reality? Pause for a moment and just breathe. Remind your soul that there is no sin so great that God has become LESS good toward you. You have no faith so great that God will become MORE good toward you. If God's goodness was dependent upon me, I would be in serious trouble. He is not the grumpy grandpa whose mood swings make us all walk around on tiptoes. We don't have to wait until he's eaten a good meal before we ask to use the car. God will never be good because of you. God is always good because of himself. I can almost see your tense shoulders release as that truth sinks in.

God is awe-fully good

There are three main Greek words that could be translated "good" in the New Testament, yet they are often translated into other terms for God's character, including kind, faithful and gracious. The best example of God being called "good" in the New Testament is in a narrative that appears in all three of the Synoptic (harmonious, similar)

Gospels. In Matthew 19:17, Mark 10:18, and Luke 18:19 we read variations on the same response from Jesus – "Why do you call me good? No one is good except God alone." The points Jesus is making should not be lost on our current generations.

Point One: though we use the word "good" for that incredibly wide range of people and things, no one but God is fully good.

Point Two: because Jesus is, indeed, fully good — Jesus is, indeed, fully God!

...we must recapture the Bible concepts of
the perfection of our God Most High!
We have lost the sense and the wonder of
His awe-fullness, His perfection, His beauty.

A.W. Tozer[5]

Somehow, the term "awful" has morphed into something negative and, often, horrific. Originally, it actually referred to something that inspired wonder and reverent fear, something that made us be full of awe in our response. Our worship begins with this simple truth – God is good. He is awe-fully good. As seen in the classic by C.S. Lewis, Susan needs to clarify something about the lion named Aslan. She wants to know about his character.

---

[5] Compiled by Ron Eggert, *Tozer on the Almighty God: A 365-Day Devotional*, Moody Publishers, 2004, 2020 edition, April 30 entry. Used by permission.

> *Wrong will be right, when Aslan comes in sight,*
> *At the sound of his roar, sorrows will be no more,*
> *When he bares his teeth, winter meets its death,*
> *And when he shakes his mane, we shall have spring again.*
> *"Aslan is a lion – the Lion, the great Lion."*
>
> *"Ooh" said Susan. "I'd thought he was a man.*
> *Is he – quite safe? I shall feel rather nervous*
> *about meeting a lion"...*
>
> *"Safe?" said Mr Beaver ...*
> *"Who said anything about safe? Course he isn't safe.*
> *But he's good.*
> *He's the King, I tell you."*
>
> **C.S. Lewis**[6]

We are full of awe because God is not "safe" in the sense of powerless weakness, but he is, most certainly, good in the midst of all of his power. I love this picture, below, in the book of Jeremiah.

> *"I will make with them an everlasting covenant,*
> *that I will not turn away from doing good to them.*
> *And I will put the fear of me in their hearts, that they may not turn from me"*
> **Jeremiah 32:40 ESV**

Isn't that a beautiful image? God is so good that he promises to not turn away from his people; he will not turn from doing good for them.

---

[6] C.S. Lewis, *The Lion, the Witch and the Wardrobe*, MacMillan Publishing, 1950, First Collier Books, 1970 edition, pp. 74-76. © copyright CS Lewis Pte Ltd 1950. Used by permission.

And he is so good that he wants his people to recognise how very awefull he is so that they do not turn from him. That is an image of a covenant relationship, which we will develop more in a later chapter. For now, capture this image of that relationship – both parties are turned toward each other. What a perfect picture of goodness.

Hugs from heaven

God IS good, but, also, God DOES good. The verse at the beginning of this chapter from Psalm 119 makes this clear. All that God does is good. And all that is good is from God. The Hebrew verb most often translated "good" is related to the adjective we've already discussed. It can involve having things go well. It can be when something causes our heart to be happy. It could also be about someone doing something skilfully or when one person is pleasant to another person. Because we are made in the image of the Creator, we are able to "do good". But, once again, the word is inadequate and overused because there is that wide range of "good"-ness. You might do something skilfully as you help encourage me. Your encouragement could be empowered by the Holy Spirit. But, no matter how lovely you are and how grateful I am, the "doing good" from you is nothing compared to the "doing good" that God does.

God's actions are good in the big things – in creation, in redemption, in our future resurrection. And God's actions are good in the small things – the call from a friend who was nudged to reach out to you and they were clueless as to why; the rose bud that opened just when your heart was closing; the rain that patters on your windows and on your parched soul. I marvel at the timing of God's good gifts. As I reflect back over my many decades, I realise that when my heart was breaking with something overwhelmingly huge, God's goodness spoke to my soul through the simplest of things. And one tiny whisper of God's goodness outweighed all of the pain I felt at that moment.

Every good and perfect gift is from above,
coming down from the Father of the heavenly lights,
who does not change like shifting shadows.
James 1:17

I call those happenings "hugs from heaven" because, well, that's what they feel like to me. When the canyon below our home fills up with rain, I sit on our Hinterland deck, listening to the rushing water slapping the rocks and I feel hugged from heaven. When I am weighted by a heavy heart because God seems to be delaying something that I thought he would do quickly and I spot a new cucumber on the cucumber plant, the delight I feel lifts my heart as if it was a hug from heaven. When one of our grown children (including spouses!) reaches a major career milestone, we all rejoice and my heart smiles because they've had a hug from heaven. When a grandchild receives the most prestigious award at their school, the award that identifies godly character in them, I see that as a hug from heaven for them. All good things, even the things we think we've earned, are really hugs from heaven. Because everything good is from above.

God's good boundaries

If you are a parent, you probably understand this truth – even God's commands are good. While we know that our children's protests can be tough on the ears and tough on our hearts, we also know that our boundaries are good boundaries. We establish them to protect our children from harm and to provide for their success. The shortest distance between two points is a straight line. However, if I want to get from New York to Los Angeles via car, a straight line won't get me there. The laws of the road, the stop signs, the traffic lights, the speed controls, the rest stops – all are there to protect me and to help me reach my destination. It is good to arrive in LA and it is good to arrive there without incident. And so it is with God's teaching for us. Psalm 119: 39b-40a says, "for your laws are good. How I long for your precepts." God's directives are for our good because God is good.

Good in the not-good

There is one more aspect of God's goodness that we should address. That is the reality that God accomplishes good, even from other's evil motivations and evil actions. Old Testament Joseph teaches us this truth in rather profound ways. The short summary of what can be found in Genesis, chapters 37 - 40, is this: Joseph, who wears a colourful robe as evidence that he is the favoured son of his father, rather foolishly tells his brothers about some dreams he had in which they were all bowing down to him. Unsurprisingly, they don't like hearing about those dreams and their resentment of Joseph increases all the more. Some want to kill him and some want to leave him for dead, so, together, they decide to sell their brother into slavery in Egypt.

In spite of some downturns in the story (including time in prison), Joseph finds ultimate favour in each endeavour in Egypt. By the time he is the top administrator in all of Egypt, some of those brothers are driven by famine to seek help in this neighbouring land where Joseph now lives. Fast forward to the big ending and we see his brothers cowering in fear when they realise the identity of this powerful man of Egypt. Here stands the brother they hated so much that they tried to get rid of him. And then we hear Joseph say, in Genesis 50:20[7], that what they intended to bring harm to him, God intended for good in order to accomplish the saving of many lives. God's ultimate purposes are good. Always.

And we know that in all things God works for the good of those who love him, who have been called according to his purpose.
Romans 8:28

Good praises

God is so good
God is so good
God is so good
He's so good to me.

---

[7] "You intended to harm me, but God intended it for good to accomplish what is now being done, the saving of many lives." Genesis 50:20

This little children's chorus from my childhood still rings true in my soul. Such simplicity. Such reality. In Scripture, certainly there's no better place than the Psalms to be reminded of the goodness of God. And so, we'll wrap up this look at the goodness of God with some praises seen in the Psalter. Might I suggest that we linger on each verse, no matter how familiar each may seem, lest we become complacent about the truth that God is good. God's goodness is so much more than a cute, little kids' song. God's goodness is immense in its depth and vast in its breadth. His goodness is evident far and wide. God's goodness is personal. His goodness is permanent. All of these truths will become more crystallised in the chapters ahead of us. For now, let's just settle in to this simple truth: God is good.

Good and upright is the Lord;
therefore he instructs sinners in his ways.
He guides the humble in what is right
and teaches them his way.
All the ways of the Lord are loving and faithful
toward those who keep the demands of his covenant.

Psalm 25:8-10

Taste and see that the Lord is good;
blessed is the one who takes refuge in him.
Fear the Lord, you his holy people,
for those who fear him lack nothing.
The lions may grow weak and hungry,
but those who seek the Lord lack no good thing.

Psalm 34:8-10

Give thanks to the Lord, for he is good; his love endures forever.
Let the redeemed of the Lord tell their story—
those he redeemed from the hand of the foe,
those he gathered from the lands, from east and west, from north and south.
Some wandered in desert wastelands,
finding no way to a city where they could settle.
They were hungry and thirsty, and their lives ebbed away.
Then they cried out to the Lord in their trouble,
and he delivered them from their distress.
He led them by a straight way to a city where they could settle.
Let them give thanks to the Lord for his unfailing love
and his wonderful deeds for mankind,
for he satisfies the thirsty and fills the hungry with good things.

Psalm 107:1-9

Give thanks to the Lord, for he is good. His love endures forever.

Psalm 136:1

The Lord is good to all;
he has compassion on all he has made.
All your works praise you, Lord;
your faithful people extol you.
They tell of the glory of your kingdom
and speak of your might,
so that all people may know of your mighty acts
and the glorious splendor of your kingdom.
Your kingdom is an everlasting kingdom,
and your dominion endures through all generations.

Psalm 145:9-13a

For Reflection

1. Without too much analysis, list the first five ideas that come to your mind that demonstrate the goodness of God in your life.

2. When has there been a time in which you doubted the goodness of God? How was that resolved? Is there a piece that is still unresolved? What steps can you take to find answers – in God's Word, with a trusted friend who knows of God's goodness? Determine when you will action those steps. Before moving on, pause to pray about any questions you have about God's goodness that are yet to be resolved. God can be trusted with your honest questions. He already knows those questions (we'll get to that later!) so give to him what IS in you, not what you think OUGHT to be in you.

3. Look, again, at Romans 8:28. We could read this to mean that God works all things for good **_to_** or **_for_** those who love God. Or, as N.T. Wright develops in **God and the Pandemic: A Christian Reflection on the Coronavirus and Its Aftermath,** it could mean that "God works all things towards ultimate good **_with_** and **_through_** those who love him" emphasis added.[8] Whether the good is FOR those who love him or the good is THROUGH those who love him, God works all things toward his ultimate good purposes. Sit with that thought for a while. Process it with a friend.

4. Using 1 Chronicles 16 as your inspiration, write your own hymn that testifies to the goodness of God in your life. Share it with someone.

2

GOD IS MERCIFUL

*When through the blood of the everlasting covenant
we children of the shadows reach at last our home in the light, we shall have
a thousand strings to our harps, but the sweetest may well be the one tuned to
sound forth most perfectly the mercy of God.*

A.W. Tozer[9]

When our kids were growing up in Alaska, one of our favourite family adventures was camping. Strangely, we waited until all three were out of the baby/toddler stage before we upgraded from a tent to a pop-up camper/caravan. For all parents of young ones, hear me on this – don't wait. We loved that pop-up and we got pretty great at the teamwork as we raced against the clock to get it all set up. My memory is that we got very close to the 4-minute mark from the time Daddy backed the camper into place to the moment we had a fully operational home-away-from-home.

On one particular trip through the middle of Alaska into Canada, we had the perfect set-up by a huge lake, Kluane Lake, in the Yukon Territory in Canada. If one can't have Alaskan halibut or Alaskan salmon, the lake trout in that lake are truly spectacular. Now, camping in these

---

[9] A.W. Tozer, *The Knowledge of the Holy*, Harper & Row, 1961, 1975 edition, p. 96.

regions is not quite like the camping experiences we've observed in Australia. Two major factors change everything – temperature and daylight. The temperatures are like a southern Queensland winter's coldest day. And the daylight is more appropriately called day-and-night light because the sun barely sets at all.

So, while it was still light but long after bedtime, I usually boiled water for a cosy warm drink before all five of us went to sleep. It was usually one of three options – basic hot chocolate, what we called "Russian Tea", which was barely tea and definitely not Russian, or something void of anything resembling nutrition that was called Hot Tang. I'm embarrassed to admit this last option as it was an orange-flavoured, disgustingly-sweet drink that I'd rather forget I ever served my family. On this particular night, the choice was Hot Tang. I had filled all five mugs with the boiling hot drink and let them sit on the table while they cooled a bit.

My daughter, Jeri, and I were in the women's bathroom and shower facility, quite a hike away from our campsite, when we heard a wail that could best be described as the sound of a wild animal caught in a trap. I assumed that was, indeed, what we were hearing but as we made our way back to our site, the volume of the wails increased. So, I broke into a run that took me to our camper. Inside was Joey, our youngest, in an agony that I've never witnessed before or since and that I will never be able to forget. The hot and sugary drink had spilled on his foot and between his toes. As my husband worked to peel off the sock, I held my young son. At some point, I realised that I was squeezing him far too hard. I believe that I wanted to encompass his body so fully that his pain would be removed from his body and transferred to mine. He did not deserve to suffer at all. I was the one who made the drink way too hot. I wanted to take his suffering on myself.

None of humankind's suffering is caused by any mistake on God's part; the mistakes are fully ours. Yet the whole ordeal became, for me, a reminder of God's mercy and grace. I wanted so desperately to remove all of Joey's suffering. I wanted to take his pain upon myself. Of course, that was not possible because I lacked the power to do anything of the sort. With God's mercy and grace, it's completely different. He sees our sin and our suffering, which we have brought on ourselves, and he is fully able to take all punishment on himself. He hears our wails, and in his mercy, grace, compassion, love and holy justice, Jesus takes the suffering and the death penalty upon himself.

I should hop to the ending of the story. Our daughter, Jeri, remembered seeing a medic sign along the road as we'd been driving south, toward the campground, earlier that day. It was quite a night as the five of us drove back north on the rough highway to that community. As it turned out, that little village had the only medical help within a 160km radius. Fortunately, the nurse was home and not out on rounds. Our vacation plans were altered considerably – no visits to the hot springs, many visits to that nurse up the highway, and lots of mini-golfing and fishing with Joey hobbling along on a heavily bandaged foot. The impact was quite significant for all of us. Jeri says that still, to this day, when she's in a new place and notices a medic sign, she gets a catch in her heart, wondering if she'll need that information later in the day. But God was merciful and gracious to us all on that trip as we exchanged our problems for his solutions. And he still is, today.

Hand-in-hand

Mercy and grace are uniquely distinct from each other yet often work hand-in-hand. Mercy is most easily explained as someone not giving someone else what is deserved. Mercy is about restraint, a holding back on a punishment that is fully justified and fully appropriate. It is used when a negative consequence of an action is reduced or even eliminated.

Grace, on the other hand, is all about an undeserved gift being given. Grace is utterly un-earned. Grace and mercy are each related to the word "favour". We'll develop this term more in the next chapter, especially as it relates to grace. For now, let's ponder the common English-language expression, "Do me a favour." In what circumstances do we tend to use that expression? Many times, when we ask for a favour, we are begging for mercy. Other times, when we ask for someone's favour, we are hoping for grace. Often, we are actually asking for both.

The hand of mercy reaches into a human life and removes a penalty, even though that penalty is completely deserved. The hand of grace reaches into a human life and bestows a gift, even though that gift is completely undeserved. We can see the two hands – the hand of mercy and the hand of grace – working together in the verses below:

> *But because of his great love for us, God, who is rich in **mercy**,*
> *made us alive with Christ even when we were dead in transgressions—*
> *it is by **grace** you have been saved.*
>
> **Ephesians 2:4-5, emphasis added**

Notice the way God's mercy is described. God is RICH in mercy; he is mercy-full. He doesn't run short of mercy. The gauge on God's mercy tank always reads "FULL"!

Pictures of God's mercy

We see mercy at work in a courtroom when a robber is before a judge. When the judge grants a minimal sentence by requiring repayment of all that was stolen without any prison time for the offender, that judge could be described as "mercy-full". A common Hebrew word that is often translated "mercy" carries an idea of bending or stooping in kindness to an inferior. In our picture of the judge and the criminal that is exactly what we see. The criminal is inferior, not in the sense of value but as a person with lesser power and authority. The judge – superior in power and authority – stoops low, so to speak, in kindness. It is a picture of empathy, of gentleness, and maybe a bit of pity.

But mercy is not simply an emotion, a stirring of a feeling. When someone is rich in mercy, that inner quality evokes an outward response. In this sense, mercy overlaps with another characteristic of God – his compassion. When someone's heart is full of mercy or compassion, they can't keep it in. This is more than a determination of the will; the emotions compel an action that is rooted in much more than a cognitive choice.

I was raised on US American football. I guess you could say that my dad put the "fan" in the label – a Niners' Fanatic! There is a brick on the walk outside the newer stadium in San Francisco that bears an inscription, which our family special-ordered as a birthday gift for Dad. (Some of the words are in Swedish, my heritage from both sides of my family. Our son, Brad, put great effort into language research to make sure that we got the Swedish just right.) For us, football has been a pretty big deal for a long time. So, imagine my glee, in the 1990s, when our family moved from Alaska to Denver, Colorado. A football city. I still love the Niners, but you can't live in the Mile High City, home to the Denver Broncos, and not start cheering for the Broncos. We lived in Denver for 10 years and I became a die-hard fan. When I'm watching a game, I cannot be silent. It's impossible. My emotions COMPEL me to cheer, shout, groan… not by a wilful choice but by inner compulsion.

That same idea of being compelled from within is present when we consider God's mercy and compassion. In Scripture we often see a verb attached to mercy such as in the cases of "show mercy" or "give mercy". Mercy is demonstrated in action. And we find petitioners to God "cry for mercy" or "beg for mercy". The needy people seek an action that demonstrates mercy because a simple stirring of emotions without the corresponding action would not suffice. It would be an incomplete mercy.

Skewed images

In the Old Testament, God's consistent mercy with his people is on full display. In the book of Judges there is a pattern that cycles through seven times, ending with the famous/infamous Samson vs. the Philistines battle. With every cycle, the pattern is repeated: blessing, sin, judgement, cries for mercy, deliverance, blessing. If you were to read Nehemiah 9 in my well-worn Bible from the 1970s, what you would first notice are the circles drawn around every "but" in the chapter. It makes it impossible to miss the frequency of the repetition of this pattern. God provided deliverance and blessing BUT... they rebelled... again... and again. Most of the chapter is a recitation of God's mercy "from everlasting to everlasting" (Nehemiah 9:5).

When we look at the stories of rebellion in the Old Testament, it is easy to make two errors in our judgement. One is a judgement on humankind and the other is a judgement about God. We can look down on the children of God because of their sinful, rebellious ways as we begin to think that WE would NEVER make the choices they made were we in similar situations. I'll be blunt. How silly of us, really. The very moment we think that way, our judgemental heart and pride proves us to be just the same as those we judge. We are equal in our sinful rebellion. Most of God's people in the Old and New Testaments thought they would never make those choices either. Just think of Peter. The verses below set up the story of one of the times that Peter's actions required mercy,

> *Peter said to him, "Lord, I am ready to go with you both to prison and to death." Jesus said, "I tell you, Peter, the rooster will not crow this day, until you deny three times that you know me.*
> **Luke 22:33-34 ESV**

And in the very same chapter, on the very same day, Peter did the very thing that he had boldly stood against.

> *Then they seized him and led him away, bringing him into the high priest's house, and Peter was following at a distance. And when they had kindled a fire in the middle of the courtyard and sat down together, Peter sat down among them. Then a servant girl, seeing him as he sat in the light and looking closely at him, said, "This man also was with him." But he denied it, saying, "Woman, I do not know him." And a little later someone else saw him and said, "You also are one of them." But Peter said, "Man, I am not." And after an interval of about an hour still another insisted, saying, "Certainly this man also was with him, for he too is a Galilean." But Peter said, "Man, I do not know what you are talking about." And immediately, while he was still speaking, the rooster crowed. And the Lord turned and looked at Peter. And Peter remembered the saying of the Lord, how he had said to him, "Before the rooster crows today, you will deny me three times." And he went out and wept bitterly.*
> **Luke 22:54-62 ESV**

Along with being judgemental toward individuals in Scripture, we can also be rather judgemental in our assessment of God's actions in the Bible, seeing God as wrathful in his justice and righteousness in the Old Testament and seeing Jesus as merciful and gracious in the

New Testament. This dichotomy could not be further from the truth. As co-existing attributes of God, God's mercy and grace are fully operative alongside his justice and righteousness. It is never "either/or" with God's mercy and justice. It is always "both/and".

Mercy AND justice

*And the Lord **regretted** that he had made man on the earth, and it **grieved** him to his heart.*
Genesis 6:6 ESV, emphasis added

From beginning to end, God's patient, loyal, merciful gracious love is revealed in the Bible. In Genesis chapter 6 we read the epic flood narrative. It might be a bit surprising to realise that the emotions of God that led to the flood did not include anger or wrath in any way. The two highlighted words used in verse 6, above, could be best translated "sorrowed" and "grieved". The Hebrew word for sorrow is translated in a variety of ways, including that God repented, changed his mind, or was sorry for making humans. But this Hebrew word conveys a heavy sighing with deep emotion. Therefore, some Bible scholars believe that this is more accurately translated "sorrow" rather than "sorry". The second word, consistently translated "grieved", would then be reinforcing the first word. So, at a time when many picture God's anger driving him to destroy humanity, we have the wrong image.

Picture, instead, the Creator grieving the choices humanity has consistently made. Even as he has offered them the gift of himself plus everything else that he can provide them, they have consistently chosen to do evil. This long-suffering of God is described in Isaiah chapter 30, verse 1. "'Ah, stubborn children,' declares the Lord, 'who carry out a plan, but not mine'" (ESV). Later in the same chapter we see that God is waiting to show his compassion and mercy; he is waiting to be gracious. He is restraining the desire to give all that is good. Because his love for us includes our free choice to respond, he will provide that mercy and grace when we are willing to obey him and receive from him.

For thus said the Lord God, the Holy One of Israel,
"In returning and rest you shall be saved;
in quietness and in trust shall be your strength."
But you were unwilling, and you said,
"No! We will flee upon horses";
therefore you shall flee away;
and, "We will ride upon swift steeds";
therefore your pursuers shall be swift.
A thousand shall flee at the threat of one;
at the threat of five you shall flee, till you are left
like a flagstaff on the top of a mountain,
like a signal on a hill.
Therefore the Lord waits to be gracious to you,
and therefore he exalts himself to show mercy to you.
For the Lord is a God of justice;
blessed are all those who wait for him.

Isaiah 30:15-18 ESV

Those of you who are parents can relate to this, I am sure, though in a non-perfect-parent way! I can remember so many times with our children, and now with our eight grandchildren, when Jim and I wanted to take them somewhere fun. An outing had been in the works. But, not wanting to use the plan as a bribe, we did not share the plan with them. It would be a surprise. The day would progress, stubbornness would raise its ugliness, warnings were given, discipline was meted out. And all the while, the outing was having to wait. It was one of those times when "this hurts us more than it hurts you" was very, very true. We had been delighted with the anticipation of their delight. But they missed out. They were not willing to obey. Even though we might have had mercy on them by not giving them all that they deserved, the outing had to wait for repentance and obedience. It was, on a human dimension, justice and mercy working side-by-side.

Now, let's consider the perfectly flawless example of the "both/and" that is found in Jesus Christ. In him, we see God's mercy and grace working hand-in-hand with God's justice and righteousness. God's righteousness required a penalty for sin while God's mercy and grace required Jesus' payment of that penalty. Somehow, to say that I'm grateful seems so inadequate.

God made him who had no sin to be sin for us,
so that in him we might become the righteousness of God.
2 Corinthians 5:21

God is merciful, still

We cannot make God's mercy non-existent. If we ignore it, it still won't go away. However, because God has given us all free choice, we can refuse to receive God's mercy and we, therefore, render it inoperable in our lives. Sadly, the Scriptures are filled with examples where humanity, collectively or individually, walked away from God's mercy. And yet… God was (and God is) still merciful.

I came to faith in Jesus as my personal Saviour at a very young age, but it took the same mercy toward me as it does toward anyone who turns to Jesus even after 70 years of rebellion and blatant sin! I was a sinner in need of the Saviour's mercy and grace. And his mercy has been at work every day of my life since that day I surrendered to Jesus. Because, as the age-old saying goes that is based upon Romans 12:1[10] – "The problem with a living sacrifice is that it keeps crawling off the altar."[11] (A chuckle might be appropriate.)

So many times, in my journey, I have found that I have slowly crawled off the altar and taken over the "god-ing" of my life. I've subtly and, sometimes, blatantly acted as though little ol' Sharon was the god of my life and the one true God was side-lined. My actions and heart implied that I could do better than God was doing at running my life. Ahhhhhh, the mercy of God as he so often spared me the consequences of my stupidity. And his grace was always ready for me as soon as I was ready to admit my foolish arrogance.

---

10 "Therefore, I urge you, brothers and sisters, in view of God's mercy, to offer your bodies as a living sacrifice, holy and pleasing to God—this is your true and proper worship." Romans 12:1.
11 Attributed to D.L. Moody, 1837–1899, evangelist and writer, founder of Moody Church, Moody Bible Institute, and Moody Press.

We'll head into the amazing wonders of God's grace in our next chapter. But let's sit a bit longer with the reality of God's mercy. We know not the hundreds or thousands of times God's mercy has stooped down into our mess and spared us pain and suffering – pain and suffering that our childish behaviour actually earned and deserved.

But when the kindness and love of God our Savior appeared, he saved us,
not because of righteous things we had done,
but because of his mercy.

Titus 3:4-5a

For Reflection

1. Think back over your own story of God's cycle of mercy. When have you experienced the pattern of blessing, sin, judgement, cries for mercy, deliverance...? Write some thoughts about it.

2. Where are you in that cycle right now? Are you in the blessing stage? Then take a moment to praise God for the current blessings in your life. Is complacency sneaking into your life as you

grow accustomed to abundance? Or is pride rising up as you begin to think you've earned the abundance you are enjoying? Talk with God about that.

3. Maybe you're not in a season of blessing. Are you facing a current struggle? Is that struggle related to an area of your life that calls for repentance? Whatever the cause of the struggle, pray about it, now. If you are needing to repent and you don't want to do so, ask God to help you to want to want to. Yes, you read that right! Want to want to. That's what is so amazing about the mercy and grace of God – in our struggles with sin, he meets us. The Holy Spirit works within us to cause us to begin to want to want to! We are not only desperately in need of God's mercy. We are desperately in need of WANTING God's mercy.

4. Have you ever asked for God's mercy? If not, I want to invite you to do that right now. There aren't any religious hoops to jump through to become a follower of Jesus. It's not easy, but it's very simple. You just have to get honest before our God. It is simpler than you might expect because he already knows you better than you know yourself. Talk with him about the mess you're in and the mercy you seek. Thank God for the gift of Jesus who died on the cross so that the righteousness of God could pay for our unrighteousness. (See Titus 3:4-5 on the previous page). Romans 10:9 says, , 'Jesus is Lord,' and believe in your heart that God raised him from the dead, you will be saved." Tell someone about your decision.

3

GOD IS GRACIOUS

The grace of God is love freely shown towards guilty sinners, contrary to their merit and indeed in defiance of their demerit. It is God showing goodness to persons who deserve only severity, and had no reason to expect anything but severity.

J.I. Packer[12]

Every time I think of the grace of God, I can hear my dad's voice, "Sharon, God has shown his grace to our family in so many ways." Or to a visitor in their home as Dad is recovering from one of many surgeries he'll say, "It's by the grace of God that I am here." As I'm writing, my father is 92 years old and living with my mom in their Alaskan home, in the midst of pandemic crises, dependent on daily care from my sister and her family. There is rarely a day that goes by that Dad doesn't turn his own attention back to the grace of God. It's been many years since we last lived in Alaska. Hearing anyone speak of God's grace takes me back there every time — at least in my heart.

The simplest way to distinguish grace from mercy is that mercy is not giving us what we do deserve and grace is giving us what we don't deserve. So, let's go back to that courtroom scene in the previous chapter.

---

[12] J.I. Packer, *Knowing God*, InterVarsity Press, © 1973 J.I. Packer. Reproduced by permission of Hodder and Stoughton, Limited, London. 1973 edition InterVarsity Press, p. 120.

Grace doesn't leave that robber free to walk out of the courtroom; that's mercy. Grace is when the judge decides to take the robber's place in jail. And, even more. Grace is the judge saying, "Here's $2,000 to help you get started with your new life."

God made him who had no sin to be sin for us,
so that in him we might become the righteousness of God.
2 Corinthians 5:21

In his book, **God Came Near**,[13] Max Lucado takes us through an astounding dialogue, which he witnessed as a young believer. It is found in the chapter entitled **Absurdity in the Flesh**. If at all possible, find a copy of this chapter and read it. I will hit the key points that, admittedly, will not do the encounter justice.

A lecturer was addressing a group when a sincerely baffled man, standing in the back of the room, a bit distanced from the others, began to ask a series of questions: "'You mean to tell me God became a baby... and that he was born in a sheep stable?... He was raised in a blue-collar home? He never wrote any books or held any offices, yet he called himself the Son of God?... And this crucifixion story... no followers came to his defense? And then he was executed like a common junkyard thief?... And... he was buried in a borrowed grave?... After three days in the grave he was resurrected and made appearances to over five hundred people?... And all this was to prove that

---

[13] Max Lucado, *God Came Near*, Thomas Nelson, 1986, 2004 edition, pp. 11-13.

God still loves his people and provides a way for us to return to him?'" To each of the questions, Landon Saunders, the lecturer, answered simply and gently with short affirmations and confirmations.

The questioning continued with one final struggle, "'Doesn't that all sound rather… doesn't that all sound rather absurd?'" To which Landon responded, "'Yes. Yes, I suppose it does sound absurd, doesn't it?'"

Then, Max Lucado explains his own struggles as he processed facing this Jesus whom he had never before seen. And the chapter concludes with these thoughts, below.

Bloodstained royalty. A God with tears. A creator with a heart.
God became earth's mockery to save his children.
How absurd to think that such nobility would go to such poverty
to share such a treasure with such thankless souls.
But he did. In fact, the only thing more absurd than the gift
is our stubborn unwillingness to receive it.

Max Lucado[14]

Is it any wonder that the most famous hymn of all time is ***Amazing Grace?***[15] The grace of God truly is amazing. And so very difficult to grasp. And even more difficult to explain. Let's take the plunge and begin to soak in the wonder of God's grace.

---

14 Ibid, p. 15.
15 John Newton, *Amazing Grace*, 1779, Public Domain.

Giving and receiving favour

---

*The Lord passed before him and proclaimed,
"The Lord, the Lord, a God merciful and gracious, slow to anger,
and abounding in steadfast love and faithfulness."*
Exodus 34:6 ESV

The Bible Project has become a terrific source of excellent Bible teaching in recent years. Their podcasts, videos and other free resources are making a huge impact in Biblical understanding across the globe. Concurrent to my work on this book, they created a new series of podcasts, videos and other resources on the very first attributes of God that are listed in Scripture. The first words God uses to describe himself are found, here, in Exodus 34:6. I highly recommend The Bible Project podcast on grace.[16]

The Hebrew word translated "grace" is rooted in another Hebrew word, which means "favour". As we saw when we looked at mercy, someone in a lower position of power or authority can find favour in the eyes of someone with great power. This kind of favour often involves a gift. The gift could be earned. But not necessarily. And when it is unearned, it is our Biblical understanding of grace.

As promised when we looked at God's mercy, let's now dig into the concept of favour – a thought that is very much embedded in the meanings of both mercy and grace. Think of the ways we use the

---

[16] The Bible Project, https://bibleproject.com/podcast/the-uniquely-biblical-view-of-grace. Used by permission.

word in English. Some parents struggle with having a favourite child. (Though some in our family try to teasingly prove otherwise, every one of my children and grandchildren are my favourites!) Joseph was the favoured son of Jacob, who became known as Israel. Israel had twelve sons who each became the father of one of the twelve tribes in the nation of Israel. Having a favourite son proved to be hazardous to Jacob and his boys. Bragging about being the favoured son proved to be hazardous to Joseph. But just as for Joseph, being favoured comes with benefits.

Sometimes someone who does not deserve favour seeks that favour or grace from someone who has power over them. Jacob, before being renamed Israel, was known as The Deceiver. Twenty years after cheating his brother, Esau, out of the birthright that justly belonged to Esau, Jacob sought favour from Esau (Genesis 32:5). Imagine this situation – Esau had no knowledge of Jacob's whereabouts all this while. Esau had remained home with the family, carrying on the responsibilities of the firstborn son, even as he lived without the blessing of the firstborn. Into that scenario arrives messengers from Jacob who are seeking Esau's favour over Jacob and his household. No number of gifts to remove past deeds could pay the price of the stolen birthright. To give that kind of favour Esau needed grace. Lots of it. And Esau gave Jacob undeserved grace. Jacob found favour in Esau's eyes.

So, Jacob and his entire household returned to the land of his father in Canaan. And at the very place where God had revealed himself to Jacob twenty years earlier as Jacob was fleeing from his angry brother (Genesis 28), the very place Jacob had renamed Bethel (meaning house of God) because God had met him there, God again appeared to Jacob and changed his name from Jacob – The Deceiver – to Israel – One Who Wrestled with God (Genesis 32). And this man, this one who had been a deceiver, found favour in God's eyes. Through Israel and his twelve sons came all twelve tribes of this nation that would be called Israel. That's grace. Amazing grace.

Hyper-grace

The law was brought in so that the trespass might increase. But where sin increased, grace increased all the more, so that, just as sin reigned in death, so also grace might reign through righteousness to bring eternal life through Jesus Christ our Lord.
Romans 5:20-21

The presence of the law helped to display the heavy strength of sin. Have you ever gone to a paint shop to match a colour on your ceiling that you called "white"? It's rather revealing! Prior to the paint shop visit, you might have thought your ceilings were white. After viewing all of the options, you realise that your ceiling colour is what you, regretfully, now call dirty white. It just looks so dingy next to a stark white. And at this paint shop you learn that there's yellow-white, cream, grey-white, blue-white... the options are endless. The law is similar to that stark white paint. It has no tint, no coloured base. Next to the law, we place our sample from our ceiling paint we called "white" and it reveals the absolute dinginess of our own righteousness.

There's an amazing phrase in this passage that deserves a closer look – "where sin increased, grace increased all the more." The original language says, basically – where sin abounded, grace hyper-abounded or super-abounded. In other words, we can't out-sin God's grace. There is no sin for which God's grace is not greater. No matter the colour of our paint, so to speak, God's grace is super. We cannot out-do God's super-dooper grace. Amazing.

Grace, works, or effort

It is pretty astounding how easily we get things mixed up when it comes to our daily walk with God. Most of us, some easily and some after many years of confusion, get to the place where we realise that we are saved by grace, alone, through faith, alone.

---

*For it is by grace you have been saved, through faith—
and this is not from yourselves, it is the gift of God—
not by works, so that no one can boast.*
Ephesians 2:8-9

But why do so many recognise that we come to a relationship with God through the death and resurrection of the Son, by God's grace, through faith... and then we think we stay in that relationship through works?! Dear friends (I feel like we're friends at this point), if works can't save you, works can't keep you. It's that plain and it's that simple.

Works are the things we do that demonstrate our "merit" or our worthiness in an attempt to gain a relationship with God. Most religions are packed with works, all of which are quite impossible to pull off. But here's where it sometimes gets confusing. Two people can do the same thing and for one it is "works" while for the other it is, what I will call, "effort". The major difference is where that action stands on a timeline in relationship to the cross of Christ. If it is BEFORE the cross, before we have a relationship with God through trusting in the gift of Jesus, then it is works. If it is AFTER the cross, after we have a relationship with God through the grace of Jesus and we now are growing in grace, then it is effort.

Okay, I hear alarm bells going off. And there are so many places to go to get that alarm to stop. Let's start with an illustration. Here's a classic one – helping an old lady across the street. Gentleman A (for anyone who takes care of an old lady is most certainly a gentleman or a gentlewoman) is wanting to please God in order to earn his salvation. So, he regularly looks for old ladies that need help crossing the street. In his eagerness, he might even hang out on busy street corners so that he can quickly add points to his "merit column". His works are all for naught. They are filthy rags.

---

*All of us have become like one who is unclean,
and all our righteous acts are like filthy rags;
we all shrivel up like a leaf, and like the wind
our sins sweep us away.*
Isaiah 64:6

Gentleman B is living his life as a disciple of Jesus Christ. He is a Christian, saved by grace through faith. Out of the abundance that he has received and which he daily receives, he wants to give. Now, some days, he doesn't feel like giving. But because of Christ, the One he follows, he will give when he has the opportunity. Therefore, he gladly – not because he's forced, but sometimes with great effort – walks the lady across the street. He's not doing it to GAIN anything. He's doing it as a result of what he has already RECEIVED.

Each of you should give what you have decided in your heart to give,
not reluctantly or under compulsion,
for God loves a cheerful giver.
2 Corinthians 9:7

Now some of you might be saying, "But wait, there is a Scripture verse that talks about works being a good thing." I can think of at least one verse you might be considering.

Therefore, my dear friends, as you have always obeyed—
not only in my presence, but now much more in my absence—
continue to work out your salvation with fear and trembling,
for it is God who works in you to will and to act in order to fulfill his good purpose.
Philippians 2:12-13

There are two reasonable ways to interpret this passage and each has nothing to do with works. A look at the Greek word that is translated "work out" helps us see that it's not relating to merit but to completing something, to finish this walk as a disciple of Jesus Christ with seriousness, with commitment and with effort. Another interpretation involves bringing what is inside to the outside, to have outward expressions of the truth of our salvation that is internal, to make our salvation a fully integral loop or circuit, to bring it out or work it out so that it is complete. This, also, has nothing to do with merit or human works.

The "fear and trembling" part of the verse does not refer to any panic that could be brought on by a worry that our salvation isn't settled. I would, most certainly, tremble in fear if my salvation was dependent upon my works because my works are tarnished by sin and feeble, at best. Hallelujah that my salvation by grace through faith is not based upon me at all. So, this fear is not because of worry but is, rather, rooted in a reverence and respect for the amazing grace that is provided by the cross of Christ. This grace motivates me, with intense urgency, to a level of surrender to the Holy Spirit that will bring this truth to an authentic expression in my visible life.

This passage in Philippians serves as a reminder of the tension between the "now" and the "not yet", the "while I'm waiting, I'm not waiting".[17] I believe in the finished work of Christ on the cross. I know that our salvation is a completed work because of Jesus. And yet, this salvation is being completed every day that we draw breath, every day that we grow in grace, as our very lives demonstrate the salvation that is finished in Christ.

---

[17] *As It Is (In Heaven)*, Words and Music by Joel Houston & Ben Fielding, © 2016 Hillsong Music Publishing. Used by permission.

How is this so? The key is in the next phrase - "for it is God who works in you". Because our salvation is by grace through faith, it is God who works within us to help us obey him. Now, this is where I get gobsmacked every time. God has saved me, my works have nothing to do with that. And God keeps me, my works have nothing to do with that. But, brace yourself – God tells me to obey and then gives me the power, that is not of myself, to be able to obey. It is God who is at work within me. Not me. Romans 8:1 says, "There is therefore now no condemnation to those who are in Christ Jesus, who do not walk according to the flesh, but according to the Spirit" (NKJV). The Holy Spirit empowers us to walk in his guidance and power.

I hope you're grasping the significance of this. God wants a relationship with each of us, his creations. He says that we can't do anything to gain that relationship. He does it all in the cross of Christ Jesus. And then he says, "Okay, Sharon, you have one thing. Just one thing to do. You need to obey me." And before I can grasp the impossibility of that task he says, "But when he, the Spirit of truth, comes, he will guide you into all the truth" (John 16:13a). The Holy Spirit is our source of power to be able to obey.

This brings us to the idea of discipleship and the spiritual disciplines. A disciple is a follower. Jesus was not the first spiritual leader to have disciples. But he was the only perfect discipler! A Christ-follower is a disciple of Jesus Christ. And as disciples of Christ, we can, and must, be involved in spiritual disciplines. The best definition I've ever known for a spiritual discipline is this: something we can do, by direct effort, that enables us to do what we can't do by direct effort. We know we are supposed to be loving. After all, it's in the list of the fruit of the spirit.[18] But no tree can produce fruit by its own effort. Imagine hearing a grunting noise the next time you walk past a peach tree. Imagine that the poor tree was trying to produce peaches. Tragic, really. It forgot who it was supposed to be and what it was supposed to do.

So, if I cannot become more loving by direct effort (and let me verify that, after these many years, I have proven that to be true) then what can I do? Ah, the spiritual disciplines. I CAN be in the Word of God every day. I CAN pray. I CAN memorise Scripture, practice solitude, fast, meditate on Scripture day and night, and a host of other practices. And while I am, by direct effort, doing those practices, God's Spirit takes over my life and begins a work of transformation. That, my friends, is grace.

By exalting my own effort and striving for my own accomplishments, I insult his grace and steal the credit that belongs to him alone.

Charles Swindoll[19]

---

18 "But the fruit of the Spirit is love, joy, peace, forbearance, kindness, goodness, faithfulness, gentleness and self-control. Against such things there is no law." Galatians 5:22-23.
19 Charles Swindoll, *The Grace Awakening*, Thomas Nelson, 1990, 2010 edition, p. 19.

The grace-gift-thanks link

> *Those who suppose that the doctrine of God's grace tends to encourage moral laxity ... are simply showing that, in the most literal sense, they do not know what they are talking about. For love awakens love in return; and love, once awakened, desires to give pleasure; and the revealed will of God is that those who have received grace will henceforth give themselves to "good works" and gratitude will move any man who has truly received grace to do as God requires.*
>
> **J.I. Packer**[20]

In the New Testament, the word most often translated "grace" is **charis,** which means "gracious gift" and is the source of the English words, charisma and charismatic. I have a daughter-in-law whose name is Karissa. Her parents (and my friends since long before she was born) named her well. I've witnessed her grace at work toward her effervescent children; I've seen her give grace to others in sometimes awkward moments; I've been impacted by the grace she has offered me on many-an-occasion. She is a gift. This word is the root of another group of words that include "eucharist" – remembering the Lord's death until he comes back again, thanking God for his grace through participating in what we often call Communion or The Lord's Supper. Actually, **eucharisteo** means "giving thanks".

Think of the expression that is used for praying before we eat a meal – "saying grace". (That phrase intrigues me as to its origin. Researching the etymology of the phrase has not produced anything definitive though it appears that it might refer to conferring a blessing over the food to be eaten – sanctifying the food, so to speak.) When we talk about saying grace, the meaning is much deeper than simply thanking God for our meal. Being thankful for anything God provides is always a good place to start. But let's not stop with that most basic of habits. Our very lives can "say grace" when we live our lives out of a thankful and grace-giving heart.

God requires nothing greater from us than giving thanks.
Giving thanks is a more acceptable service than all sacrifices.
God is continually heaping innumerable benefits...
Ingratitude, therefore, is intolerable.

John Calvin[21]

Calvin might say it rather harshly for our ears, today, but his point is truth well spoken. Every day we draw breath, no matter how difficult that breath might be, is a gift. We aren't told to thank him FOR the difficulties. But we are told to thank him IN the difficulties.

---

[21] John Calvin, *John Calvin's Bible Commentaries On Genesis 24-50*, Jazzybee Verlag, 2017 edition, p. 18.

> *...give thanks in all circumstances;*
> *for this is God's will for you in Christ Jesus.*
> **1 Thessalonians 5:18**

I love the phrase "in the midst". Right smack in the middle of life, God's grace is real and it is available to me and to you. Whatever your "in the midst" might be right now… are you in the midst of waiting, in the midst of anguish, in the midst of loneliness…? God's grace is there. In the midst.

> *I know there is poor and hideous suffering, and I've seen the hungry and the guns that go to war. I have lived pain, and my life can tell: I only deepen the wound of the world when I neglect to give thanks for early light dappled through leaves and the heavy perfume of wild roses in early July and the song of crickets on humid nights and the rivers that run and the stars that rise and the rain that falls and all the good things that a good God gives.*
> **Ann Voskamp**[22]

---

[22] Ann Voskamp, *One Thousand Gifts*, Zondervan, 2011, p. 58.

For Reflection

1. Read Ephesians 1:3 through 2:10. List the ways "grace" is used and list the important words that are part of our benefits as recipients of God's grace. Take some time to praise God for his amazing grace.

2. Think about the times in this very week that God's grace has reached into your life. What can you do to notice his grace more regularly? What can you do to thank him more genuinely?

3. If you haven't, yet, listen to The Bible Project's podcast, ***The Uniquely Biblical View of Grace.***[23] It might require a few listens as it is packed with treasures of wisdom and insight. Take good notes. For a shorter adventure with The Bible Project, watch the video on God's Grace found on YouTube or on their website. Notes are recommended for this, too! Or watch it with a friend or a small group. Process it together. Finally, using your notes from those tools, explain God's grace in your own words. Paint a picture of his grace that is easy to share with someone who needs that encouragement.

4. How can you live your life in such a way that you are "saying grace" each day? Give this one some serious meditation.

---

[23] The Bible Project, *The Uniquely Biblical View of Grace*, 2020, https://bibleproject.com/podcast/series/character-of-god. Used by permission.

4

GOD IS COMPASSIONATE

Yet the Lord longs to be gracious to you;
therefore he will rise up to show you compassion.
For the Lord is a God of justice.
Blessed are all who wait for him!

Isaiah 30:18

Therefore the Lord longs to be gracious to you,
And therefore He waits on high
to have compassion on you.
For the Lord is a God of justice;
How blessed are all those who long for Him.

Isaiah 30:18 NASB

The story is told of a little boy who was taken to a Paderewski concert by his mother. Whether based in reality or legend, the story does illustrate a truth, so let's go ahead with it! His mother wanted to inspire her son to practise for his piano lessons, so the concert seemed to be a perfect motivator. Before the concert began, while the mother was engaged in a conversation with others nearby, the boy slipped away as he was magnetically drawn to the truly grand piano on the stage. He sat down at that piano and began to play the simplest of all pointer-finger-only songs – **Chopsticks.**

Imagine the noise of the audience as it changed from quiet conversations to growing grumblings and complaints about the very presence of such a young boy at such a refined place. When hearing the piano and the murmurings of the audience, Ignace Paderewski is said to have calmly moved to the piano and sat down beside the child. With arms of kindness, he reached around the boy and began playing beautiful additions to the boy's simple tune, whispering to him all-the-while, "Keep playing. Don't stop. Keep playing. Don't stop." What a beautiful picture of God's compassion toward humanity. He sees the mess we've made of things. He hears the results. His heart is stirred. He stoops down on our level, offers his hands of mercy and grace, and makes beauty out of our seriously weak **Chopsticks.**

God's first description of himself

As mentioned in a previous chapter, in Exodus 34:6 we read the first words that God ever uses to describe himself to his people. The very first word of this grouping is our theme for this chapter – compassion. So, what is meant by "compassion" in the Bible? When is the word used to describe God and when is it used for humankind? And how does it differ from mercy? Let's dig in!

Notice the verse at the beginning of this chapter. I've presented two different translations of the same verse. So many times, we miss out on the understanding of the original text of Scripture so let's unpack it a bit by reading these two translations. The same Hebrew word is used for God's longing for (or waiting for) those on whom he wants to show compassion as is used for the blessing that comes to those who long for (or wait for) God. When we looked at God's mercy, we read more of the surrounding verses of this passage. My point, here, is that in his waiting for us to obey, God has a strong longing, a strong desire to exemplify who he is in his action. He isn't just compassionate within himself, he longs to GIVE compassion to each of us, his creations.

Mercy and compassion

We considered, when focusing on the mercy of God, that mercy and compassion overlap. Sometimes, the same word in the original language of Scripture is translated "mercy" and sometimes it is translated "compassion". However, there are different nuances within the use of each word. The English word, compassion, refers to a stirring of emotion, when seeing the unfortunate conditions of another, which is accompanied by a desire to help. Notice that compassion is an emotion that arises when seeing another's misfortunes whereas, as we saw earlier, mercy is an emotion that arises when seeing another's misdeeds. The misfortunes do not deserve discipline, the misdeeds do.

We have compassion toward a child who is a victim of abuse. Victims are always undeserving of suffering. In direct contrast, perpetrators are always deserving of punishment. We must offer compassion to the victim while we might offer mercy to the perpetrator of that abuse. Each situation involves an emotional response. The distinction is that mercy always relates to a result or punishment that is, in actuality, well deserved. Compassion is the offering of a hand of loving help; mercy is the restraining of a hand of judgement.

Hebrew: womb

The major Hebrew word, which is translated "compassion" is linked to the Hebrew word for "womb". Again, I refer you to The Bible Project and their excellent resources on the attributes of God, which we see in Exodus 34:6.[24] The beauty of this word, compassion, is seen as "the tender feelings of a mother for her vulnerable infant." The word can be translated "deeply moved" and we see that usage in 1 Kings 3:16-28. This is the fascinating demonstration of the wisdom of King Solomon when two women were each claiming the same baby as their own son. When the king determined that the baby should be divided in half for the two women, the true mother was deeply moved. In her compassion toward her son, she begged for his life and offered her son to the other woman. The deceitful woman clearly had no compassion. The true mother was easily identified. The dilemma was resolved.

The woman whose son was alive was deeply moved out of love for her son and said to the king, "Please, my lord, give her the living baby! Don't kill him!" But the other said, "Neither I nor you shall have him. Cut him in two!"

1 Kings 3:26

This same concept is used to describe God's compassion in the book of Isaiah.

[24] The Bible Project, https://bibleproject.com/explore/video/character-of-god-compassion. Used by permission.

> *"Can a woman forget her nursing child, that she should have no compassion on the son of her womb? Even these may forget, yet I will not forget you."*
> **Isaiah 49:15 ESV**

God's love involves a motherly compassion. Of course, his compassion is also perfect compassion. Though it may seem impossible to our sensibilities, a mother might be capable of forgetting her love for her child; God will never forget his children. In Isaiah, we see God's promise that he will provide for the salvation of his people. Because compassion is not just an emotion, God will make a way.

Compassion in action

God will make a way… in Jesus. Just as in the book of Isaiah, in the book of Matthew we see Jesus expressing his longing to move with compassion, if only the people would be willing to receive it.

> *"O Jerusalem, Jerusalem, the city that kills the prophets and stones those who are sent to it! How often would I have gathered your children together as a hen gathers her brood under her wings, and you were not willing!"*
> **Matthew 23:37 ESV**

Two distinct Greek words are used in the New Testament, one for mercy and one for compassion. There are many examples of these two words in the Gospel of Luke. Compassion is the term in Luke 7:13[25] when Jesus sees the widow at Nain who has lost her son. In Luke 15:20,[26] in what is typically called the parable of the prodigal son though it is more of a parable of the loving father, the same term is used for what the father feels as he runs toward his son who is returning home after being gone for far too long.

Mercy is the term used when describing God's faithful, covenantal love toward humankind as God provides a way for our salvation. This is evident in Luke 1 in the hymn sung by Mary and in the hymn sung by Zechariah. God's mercy toward his people results in jubilant praise with the news of the arrival of Jesus Christ to needy humanity.

An object lesson

One summer in the early 1990s, God gave our family a beautiful picture of his compassionate care for us. We had a neighbour lady who worked so hard to attract birds to her yard with bird houses, bird feeders and even a bird bath. If not for the bird food that sat in the feeders, awaiting the birds, the feeders would have been completely empty. No bird stayed. As far as I'm aware, no bird even visited. So, imagine my surprise when I realised that we had a robin that chose to nest in one of our hanging fuchsia baskets on our front porch.

This was what I would call a lazy porch. It was long and deep, well

---

[25] "When the Lord saw her, his heart went out to her and he said, 'Don't cry.'" Luke 7:13.
[26] "So he got up and went to his father. But while he was still a long way off, his father saw him and was filled with compassion for him; he ran to his son, threw his arms around him and kissed him." Luke 15:20.

shaded, and able to hold many flowers in the window boxes and the hanging baskets. I loved the flowers, but my favourite feature was the porch swing on the far end of the porch. I could spend many-an-hour just wondering as I rocked in that swing. Hence the label – a lazy porch. Life was slow and easy to handle on our porch. Maybe that's what created a welcome space for Mother Robin.

As it became apparent that Mother Robin was sitting on eggs, we chose to leave the swing alone and peek at progress from inside the house. While sitting in my "quiet time chair" one morning, I was meditating on the passage in Psalm 46:10, "Be still and know that I am God." Other translations read, "cease striving". As I was contemplating what God was saying to me about trusting him rather than trying to do it all myself, Mother Robin flew in with breakfast for her chicks. I watched with delight as a few tiny beaks popped up out of the flowers and allowed their mother to fill their mouths with treats. It was as if God was saying, "See how much I care about you, Sharon. Just as this mother cares for her chicks, I care for you. I know that you're helpless without me. That's why I provide."

Sometimes our circumstances can smother the truth. It might seem like God cares for you much less than any mother robin cares for her chicks. But the truth remains – God is compassionate toward you. That lazy summer day, God was so gentle in his compassion to me. When I was busy fretting over something in that season that I've since forgotten, God gently reminded me that it was not my job to leave the nest and forage for food. It was my job to receive from God the provisions that he compassionately gave.

A broken heart

It seems that with each generation, we learn more and more about how our thinking, emotions and physical conditions are intricately linked. Did you know that there is actually a medical diagnosis called Broken Heart Syndrome? The scientific name is takotsubo cardiomyopathy, being first described in 1990 in Japan. It is named after an octopus trap. An online search will guide you to further information about this syndrome in which surging stress hormones essentially stun the heart for a time and often mimic symptoms of a heart attack.

This points to the fascinating nature of our complex bodies. Our emotions do not stand alone; they are intricately linked to our bodies. Of course, the syndrome of a broken heart is brought on, most often, by personal stressors and traumatic events in which we are personally involved. Yet, this word "compassion" involves some level of deep involvement, both emotionally and physically, because of stressors and traumatic events that don't affect us, directly, but are incredibly impactful for someone else beyond ourselves.

Then Jesus made a circuit of all the towns and villages. He taught in their meeting places, reported kingdom news, and healed their diseased bodies, healed their bruised and hurt lives. When he looked out over the crowds, his heart broke. So confused and aimless they were, like sheep with no shepherd.
Matthew 9:35-37 MSG

Eugene Peterson chooses the expression "his heart broke" when describing what is often translated "moved with compassion". The Greek word used here is fascinating because it is linked to our inward parts – our heart, lungs, kidney, liver, bowels. Our attempts to describe this in the English language bring out phrases such as: "our heart aches", "it hit us in the gut", "that really cuts deep". When Jesus saw the needs of lost humanity, it hurt him deeply. But godly compassion does not end with a broken heart; that's only the beginning. Jesus was "moved" with compassion. See the response of Jesus in the next verse:

> *"What a huge harvest!" he said to his disciples. "How few workers! On your knees and pray for harvest hands!"*
> **Matthew 9:38 MSG**

This is true compassion – a stirring of emotion, which leads to a response. And how did Jesus say we should respond? Pray! What a great way to launch our response. Compassion causes us to want to DO something. And the first something we should do is to pray. Compassion might cause us to say, "Oh, what a pity!" but to be godly compassion it must be followed by, "How can I help?"

For Reflection

1. Pause to contemplate God's compassion toward you. It's personal. You aren't just getting in on a group rate because God loves the world. If you dare, write out a love letter from God to you, including his words of compassion toward you this day.

2. Has there been a time that something happened in your life that you know was directly linked to God's compassion toward you? Spend some time praising God for the many ways his compassion has impacted your daily life. Tell someone about the ways God has shown compassion to you. Encourage them to do the same.

3. Think back on a time that you were "moved with compassion". What action did you take as a result?

4. How can you be a bearer of God's compassion in your world right now? If you are not "moved", ask God to help you to want to want to. Let praying launch your compassionate actions.

5

GOD IS PATIENT

[Patience] differs from mercy in the formal consideration of the object: mercy respects the creature as miserable, patience respects the creature as criminal; mercy pities him in his misery, and patience bears with the sin which engineered the misery and is giving birth to more.

Stephen Charnock [27]

So much of what we have begun to unpack points us to another attribute of God that we will soon be discussing at length. But before we get to that word, there's another character of God that must be addressed. So be patient, we'll get to God's love soon!

Patience. That's a tough attribute for us to embrace for ourselves. We are, after all, so very impatient. I am, at least. And I believe I am not alone. A dear friend once made a sign for me that is situated in a place of prominence in our home. It says, "Still, be still!" I needed it, then. I need it, now. Usually my patience sounds like this – "God, I'm being patient, so please hurry up!" And so many times God patiently says to me, "Sharon – still, be still." We are so different in so many ways, God and I. (An understatement, to be sure!) Patience is only one way of many.

Look at God's history of patience with us. Our God who is fully good, out of his great compassion, offered us mercy and grace at the cross. But, not just at the cross. Not only did Jesus, God's one and only Son, suffer unspeakable pain when he hung on that cross where you and I deserved to be, but his very arrival on earth was a point of suffering. For the perfect, spotless Lamb of God to come to take away the sins of the world meant that he chose to live AS a human WITH humans for over 30 years. Amazing, really. And at the cross the Father suffered a broken relationship with his only Son as the wrath of God was poured out on our sins, which Jesus bore.

The next day John saw Jesus coming toward him and said,
"Look, the Lamb of God, The next day John saw Jesus coming
who takes away the sin of the world!"
John 1:29

He himself bore our sins in his body on the tree,
that we might die to sin and live to righteousness.
By his wounds you have been healed.
1 Peter 2:24 ESV

What did God get in return? Well, he got children who were (and are) selfish, petty, demanding, argumentative, critical, unkind, unsatisfied, ungrateful.... Right? Patience is a part of God's suffering.

In fact, in some Bible translations the word for "patience" is rendered "long-suffering". We were sinners when Christ died for us. He redeemed us in our sin and he continues to forgive us as we sin. When we place our trust in Jesus and enter into a relationship with God, we are no longer called sinners. But we are most certainly capable of sin. And we certainly do sin.

At centres

But God demonstrates his own love for us in this:
While we were still sinners, Christ died for us.
Romans 5:8

When our kids were young, Jim and I led a pre-school-aged, midweek program at our church. It was heavily wrapped around Bible memorisation, something that could become a bit legalistic as it involved ticking boxes, yet something that I wish was more in vogue in our lives as disciples of Jesus, today. I still smile when I think of this verse, Romans 5:8 where, in the King James Version it reads, "... while we were yet sinners, Christ died for us." One evening, a precious, little five-year-old arrived to our meeting fully prepared to recite this verse, which she had worked so hard to learn. And she proudly said, "While we were at centres, Christ died for us." Well, we had to have a wee chat, she and I, about what the verse actually said and, more importantly, what it meant. But a little while later I thought about her again and realised that she wasn't that off base.

Children, by that time in educational history, had grown very accustomed to "centres" – little stations where about five children can gather at a time. Centres are places where children can enrich their learning experiences, reinforce the big idea of the lesson, or just have a great time playing. At centres, children remain happily busy. Often, they are so engrossed in their fun that when it's time to rotate centres, they absolutely refuse. And that's where her theology was pretty accurate! Humankind gets quite busy with our little activities, our learning centres. We think our little world is life, itself. Our meaning becomes wrapped up in the activity. And when our attention is drawn away from our "centre" to something bigger, we complain. Because we are not just AT centres, we BECOME the centre, the centre of our universe. While we were at centres, Christ died for us. Oh, the patience of God, to die for totally distracted, self-centred humanity.

Pondering patience

I wonder as I wander out under the sky
How Jesus the Savior did come for to die
For poor, orn'ry people like you and like I
I wonder and I wander,
Out under the sky
Annie Morgan[28]

Have you ever wondered about the patience of God? I most certainly have. We've had, since our children were school-aged, a histomap of

[28] Annie Morgan, collected by John Jacob Niles, 1933, lyrics: Public Domain.

World History. It's a long and narrow chart that reaches from floor to ceiling, displaying the rise and fall of empires for approximately 4000 years. Each civilisation's impact is represented by the length and width of a designated-colour section, portraying that civilisation's longevity and breadth. It doesn't require attention to every detail to realise how often history has repeated itself in its theme and variations.

While I was homeschooling Joey in high school, we encountered an out-of-print copy of Sir John Glubb's book, **The Fall of Empires and Search for Survival.**[29] Glubb demonstrates a repeated pattern in each "empire" as it rises and then falls, tracing six periods through many of history's greatest societies. The six periods are: The Age of Pioneers, The Age of Conquest, The Age of Commerce, The Age of Affluence, The Age of Intellectualism, The Age of Decadence. It's a fascinatingly insightful book, which could cause us to learn much from history. Humanity does not often have the courage to correct the very history we tend to repeat.

There can be no doubt that too long a period
of power and wealth leads to decadence.
Sir John Glubb[30]

And yet. And yet, God is patient. In Genesis 1 we read the account of the creation of our world. In Genesis 3, we see the entrance of sin into the previously perfect creation. And by Genesis 6, we see

[29] Sir John Glubb, *The Fall of Empires and Search for Survival*, William Blackwood and Sons, 1978.
[30] Ibid, p. 03.

the destruction of a very destructive humanity. In just six chapters of that recorded history, we see perfection destroyed by sin, we see humanity carrying on with life without God, we see wickedness abound, and we see God's grace upon one segment of humanity that was righteous. Wow, that didn't take long. Six chapters. Just a few generations. From our distant perspective on that history, it makes no sense to choose rebellion over obedience. Yet... they did. And, yet... we do, too.

And the rest of the Bible consistently shows an incredibly patient Creator waiting on his creation to come to their senses, so to speak.

Slow to anger

The Lord is not slow in keeping his promise, as some understand slowness. Instead he is patient with you, not wanting anyone to perish, but everyone to come to repentance.
2 Peter 3:9

The above verse reminds us that God is not slow. Though it may seem that way to us, he is not slow in keeping his promises. Think about this for a moment. When we are believing God for some breakthrough in our lives, and we wait, sometimes impatiently, we might think God is slow. In reality, one of the few ways in which God IS slow is in his anger, not in his goodness. With his patience, he is withholding the consequences that humanity justly deserves.

In Exodus 34:6, a verse we have discussed a bit already, we read that God is "slow to anger". Once again, I refer you to The Bible Project as they discuss this concept at length in some podcasts and have a valuable video on the phrase.[31] The phrase is actually a Hebrew idiom that means "long nose". Idioms are generally lost in translation, so the baffling nature of this phrase is no surprise. But consider how we picture someone who is very angry. A cartoonist might depict the person with steam or heat rising from their head. Or their face might be very red. That's not too far from the Hebrew understanding – a nose that burns hotly. So, an angry person is "hot nosed" and, therefore, a patient person is "long nosed"! It takes a patient person a very long time for their nose to get hot. When we look into God's justice, we'll come back to this idea and take it further. For now, be patient! (I write that with a grin.) The point is that God is not, in any way, quick to anger. The Creator is, in fact, incredibly patient with his creation. Unbelievably patient, actually.

Patient for repentance

Generation after generation, from the Garden of Eden to the wickedness of the immediate offspring of Adam and Eve, to the wickedness of the whole earth in Genesis 6, to the rebellion of the nation of Israel in the wilderness and then again in the Promised Land, and then in exile, and then in rebuilding Jerusalem, and to the nation of Nineveh... God patiently offers mercy. He patiently withholds consequences. He patiently offers grace. God patiently forgives. Again.

---

[31] The Bible Project, https://bibleproject.com/podcast/series/character-of-god. Used by permission.

Jim and I have eight beautiful grandchildren. They are all packed into an age-spread of less than seven years. Currently, we have two 10-year-olds, two 7-year-olds, one 6-year-old, two 4-year-olds, and one 3-year-old. Why do I mention our grands in a chapter on God's patience? I can almost hear the knowing chuckles from some of you. The answer? Because I am not God. I love these eight precious souls and there's not much I wouldn't do for them. But that's easier to say when they're in smaller groups. When all eight are together and two keep doing the very thing they know they are not supposed to do… patience is in short supply. My patience, that is.

When their behaviour is perfect, I have no lack of patience. Even when they do childish things and immediately make self-corrections, no worries. My struggle is not when their actions and attitudes match their age, even. It is when their wilfulness gets in the way of obedience. Actually, even that isn't a problem when they respond to correction and apologise. The bottom line for the limit on my patience is this – repeated, wilful disobedience without repentance. That's my bottom line because, clearly, I am not God. And sadly, I'm not always godly. Godliness doesn't lack patience when there is a lack of repentance. God waits. As we saw in 2 Peter 3:9, God wants all to come to a place of repentance. He waits for us to see our sin, own that sin, and repent of that sin. Without excuses.

Powerful, purposeful patience

The patience of God is that excellency which causes him to sustain great injuries without immediately avenging himself.
A.W. Pink[32]

Stephen Charnock, the English Puritan leader from the 1600s whose quote begins this chapter, points out a profound truth: God is patient BECAUSE he is all powerful.[33] This is the major reason we fail with our own patience. As humans, when it comes to our patience, we have very limited power over it. In other words, we are unable to restrain our IMpatience. Consider this – God is patient because his power and love and wisdom are all working together to accomplish his purposes on the earth.

What if God, desiring to show his wrath and to make known his power, has endured with much patience vessels of wrath prepared for destruction, in order to make known the riches of his glory for vessels of mercy, which he has prepared beforehand for glory,
Romans 9:22-23 ESV

God's patience is on full display here as we see that he is willing to suffer a very long time for, and he is willing to patiently wait for, those who deserve destruction. He waits for those who deserve death to

---

[32] A.W. Pink, *The Attributes of God*, Baker Book House, 1975, 2006 edition, p. 80. Used by permission.
[33] Stephen Charnock, cited by A.W. Pink, *The Attributes of God*, Baker Book House, 1975, 2006 edition, p. 80. Used by permission.

come to their senses, repent and receive his mercy. What a beautiful picture – those who were vessels, containers, vases deserving wrath are transformed into vases containing God's mercy. And it's all because of God's patience. That same patience is reviewed in the book of 1 Peter.

...when God's patience waited in the days of Noah,
while the ark was being prepared, in which a few,
that is, eight persons, were brought safely through water.
1 Peter 3:20 ESV

There is something so comforting about the old-English phrase "in the fullness of time". When the perfect time, the appointed time, the set time arrived – God acted. Jesus was born into the perfect setting, politically and spiritually and historically, to redeem humanity. From our flawed perspective, there was nothing about a weary Mary and Joseph, a stable birth, under a threatening Roman governance... that seems perfect. But it was perfect for the purposes of God.

But when the set time had fully come, God sent his Son, born of a woman,
born under the law, to redeem those under the law,
that we might receive adoption to sonship. Because you are his sons,
God sent the Spirit of his Son into our hearts, the Spirit who calls out,
*"**Abba**, Father." So you are no longer a slave, but God's child;*
and since you are his child, God has made you also an heir.
Galatians 4:4-7

Aren't you glad that God is not made in our image? God never "loses his patience". He never "gets to the end of his rope" because his power sustains him. We don't see his anger emerge when he's "run out of patience". In later chapters, we'll deal with the reality that God does not set aside his patience in order to mete out justice or to display his righteousness. God is fully able to be patient because fully able is who God is. God is patient. In everything. Everywhere. At all times.

For Reflection

1. Ponder God's patience. Take a good, long time to consider the many ways God has been patient toward you, personally. You could write about it. Or maybe record a video of your thoughts.

2. Do you remember that TV game show about becoming a millionaire? Let's borrow a phrase from that and say that it's time to "phone a friend"! In the introduction of this book, I said that most often our praises, both to and of God, need to involve others. We magnify him together. Now is a good time to do that. Tell someone else about how God has been patient in your life. Being specific helps seal the memory in your mind.

3. Do you find yourself being "short-suffering" rather than long-suffering, at times? Take some time to assess your own patience and lack of it. Humble yourself before our very patient God and talk with him about your lack. Ask him to do a transformative work in this area of practicing patience. (I just had to stop and do this, myself.)

4. Is there someone in your life who has been extraordinarily patient with you? Tell them – in person, via text, through a phone call. Thank them for their patience with you. Let them know how it has, specifically, impacted you!

6
GOD IS LOVING

*For God so loved the world that He gave His
only begotten Son, that whoever believes in Him
should not perish but have everlasting life.*

John 3:16 NKJV

When I came to the point where I was eager to place my faith and my whole life in Jesus, I was approaching the age of five. My Sunday School teacher in Homer, Alaska guided me through the process of surrendering my life to Jesus after my parents had laid the groundwork over many months. My very first memory in life (that is not influenced by looking at old photos) is from that Sunday evening when, in a little log-cabin church, the pastor asked if anyone had any testimonies to share and I jumped to my feet. While nervously twirling the edges of my skirt, I said, much too rapidly, "I asked Jesus into my heart!" and promptly sat down. The pastor was pretty certain that no one understood what I said because I put it all into a multi-syllabic single word – "Iaskedjesusintomyheart" – so he asked me to repeat it. I remember the emotions, both excitement and fear, as I stood to my feet once again and very slowly said, "I asked Jesus into my heart." Yes, I was young. But, to this day, I have never doubted God's grace and goodness in my life. I fully believe that, for as much as I understood, I embraced all that God had for me, through Jesus, on that day.

What followed was a curious season, a time packed with doubts. You see, I didn't doubt God's goodness, but I definitely doubted my own goodness. Almost every night until around age 6, as my head hit the pillow and I reflected on my day I would say, once again, "Jesus, you might not believe me, but I really want to follow you. I trust you as my Saviour." I knew that my actions of the day didn't match my image of how a follower of Jesus should look. I doubted that I actually could be a Christian since I'd blown it so much that day. And that verse that everyone loved, John 3:16? It truly brought me no comfort at all.

You see, I thought I was getting in on a group rate – God loved the whole world and I was a part of that world so... lucky me... I was included. It took a long time for me to realise that God's love was personal. For me. For you. It took a long time to understand that if I was the only human on the planet, Jesus would have died for me. He would have died for you. He did. No group rates! If you have accepted God's love for you and placed your trust in Jesus, thank him once again for such a gift. If you have never surrendered your life to Jesus... now is a good time!

Lavish attacks

*See what great love the Father has lavished on us,
that we should be called children of God! And that is what we are!
The reason the world does not know us is that it did not know him.*

1 John 3:1

This fabulous verse brings us to another story from the early years of Joey, our youngest son. Vacation Bible School, or VBS, was a really big deal when our kids were young and I led what was then called Christian Education at our church in Palmer, Alaska. One morning, in the midst of our 1992 Vacation Bible School week, our three kids were going over (aka cramming for) their memory verse for the day. Joey, who was almost five years old at the time, proudly recited his verse to me before we piled into the mini-van (ah yes, the good ol' days) and headed to a full day at church. He flawlessly recited, in an unofficial, kid-friendly paraphrase, from 1 John 3:1 – "Consider the incredible love the Father has lavished on us that we should be called children of God! And that's what we are!" And then he scrunched up his little face and said, "Mommy, what's whavished?"

"Okay, stop everything," I thought. We needed to put our schedule on hold so that Joey could grasp this truth. The last thing I wanted was to have my son get a sticker for reciting a verse that he didn't understand! I quickly asked God for help telling this precious child of mine what "lavished" meant. So, I said, "Joey, it's like God was in heaven, talking amongst himself (okay, the Trinity was an emerging comprehension stretch, to be sure) and he said, 'There's Joey Kohring.' He didn't say, 'Oh, that's right, I love him, too.' He said, 'There's Joey Kohring. I love him sooooooo much!' And it's like he reached his arms down from heaven and smothered you with hugs and kisses and hugs and kisses! He wanted you to know that he loves you that much!!"

Joey seemed to take in the new information easily and was willing to head to church with his older siblings. I prayed as I drove and I wondered, "Is this dear boy of mine grasping how much God personally loves him?"

Our crazily-packed day went off well and we returned home exhausted. I had dinner preparations to do as well as preparations for the next day of VBS and I hadn't, yet, checked in with Joey about that verse. I wanted to know what he had actually grasped, but time did not allow for a great conversation. Then we heard the garage door open as Daddy was returning from work. And as Jim entered the house from the garage, Joey hollered, "Whavish Daddy!" Jeri and Brad and I all joined Joey in smothering Jim with hugs and kisses. And my heart smiled. I knew that Joey had grasped this truth in a pretty significant way. For such a young boy, this idea of God lavishing his love on us was a pretty big deal. It's a pretty big deal at any age.

A family tradition was born that day. As with most great traditions, it began with absolutely no intentionality. We called them Lavish Attacks and any time someone thought anyone else in the family needed some extra love, they'd shout "Lavish _____!" and we'd all pounce on The Named One with our hugs and kisses. Those days lasted until our two sons decided that hugs and kisses from family members were gross. But we had a lot of good years. And the memories of those years make my heart smile to this day, mainly for two reasons – I love those kids of mine, all grown up with kids of their own, and I love to remember how personal the love of God is for you and for me.

Still

Think back to a time that someone who was very dear to you told you that you had disappointed them. We hate to disappoint those we love, right? I'd almost rather have them be angry with me instead of disappointed in me. That's probably rooted in my shaky ego and insecurity. We want those we love to think highly of us. We like having them see us as pretty terrific. I wonder why we think that way? Consider, for a moment, young love. Pedestals are in full use when dating relationships are new. One of the many problems with pedestals is that anyone who is on one usually ends up falling off. And yet, we kind of like pedestals. For a while.

Jim definitely thought I had few flaws when we were newlyweds. And I liked that. But now, after 40 years of marriage, he knows my flaws quite well. And, to my dismay, I've acquired new flaws over the years. Do I wish we were back in the honeymoon stage? No way! I'm grateful that Jim's love for me is not blind. Mature love sees quite well and loves. Still.

With God, it's even better. God sees right through me. He sees into the corners of my heart and mind. That is so comforting that it makes me want to shout some hallelujahs! Let this sink in… God will never say, "I'm so surprised by what you just thought." God is never disillusioned with you. He never thinks you are someone you're not. This is life-changing news that we need to regularly ponder. God's love is NOT blind. He has laser-like vision and he loves you. Still.

That also means that God sees your pain. He knows when you've felt overlooked, unseen, diminished, out of place. He sees your hurt. He sees the shame you are carrying, which you somehow think you deserve. And he loves you. Still.

There's one more aspect to this that is crucial to grasp. Because God's love is not blind, he sees the desire to change that is hidden way down in the corner of your heart. He sees the way you want to love your father who is not very easy to love. He sees your desire to walk away from that unhealthy habit, that addiction. Because God's love is not blind, he sees all of the potential that is in you. He loves you. Still.

You have searched me, Lord,
and you know me.
You know when I sit and when I rise;
you perceive my thoughts from afar.
You discern my going out and my lying down;
you are familiar with all my ways.
Before a word is on my tongue
you, Lord, know it completely.
You hem me in behind and before,
and you lay your hand upon me.
Such knowledge is too wonderful for me,
too lofty for me to attain.

Psalm 139:1-6

There is freedom, here. We don't need to try to impress God. When we pray, all of the "thees" and "thous" in the world won't make us seem more holy in his eyes. When we're angry with God, we don't need to pretend that we're not. We can bring to him what IS in us, not what OUGHT to be in us. Why? Because God's love is not blind. Our

English word "reveal" comes from the Latin *revelare*, meaning "again veil". With God, nothing in us is behind a veil. What freedom is available to those who realise that we cannot hide any thought, word, or wish from Almighty God. There is no need to wear an actor's mask to play a role in order to make God love us more than he does. He loves us right where we are. Just as we are. Still.

However

However, God loves us too much to leave us. He won't leave us where we are when we first meet him. We've looked at aspects of this truth previously and we'll dig into it a bit more in our next chapter. We want to be careful to not cheapen the love of God by implying that because he knows our deepest thoughts and loves us, still, that we are just fine in our sin. Remember, when we talked about God's grace, we looked into Philippians 2:12-13 and said that God is working in us to enable us to WANT to do and TO do whatever will fulfil his purposes.

Because God is loving, he doesn't leave us to do whatever we like. Imagine a parent saying they love their child no matter what the child chooses to do and then leaving that child to do whatever they please. When a parent allows a young child to eat or drink whatever they can find in the house or when they allow them to play in a busy street, it is called neglect and can easily lead to involvement of the governing authorities. Love doesn't lead to lack of boundaries and lack of guidance. Quite the opposite.

It would be unjust and unrighteous for God to leave us in the mess we were in when we met him. Because of his great love for us, he provides

Jesus to pay the penalty for our sins. And also because of his great love for us, he sent the Holy Spirit to live in, empower, and guide everyone who places their faith in Jesus. Praise God for his gracious and merciful "parenting" as he provides the advice we need, as he provides the boundaries we require, and as he provides the power to obey.

"Love" just isn't adequate: hesed

I was first introduced to the Hebrew word **hesed** (pronounced with a guttural "kh"; "kh-esed") when I was about 19 years old and in Bible College in Portland, Oregon. Our theology professor, David C. Needham, possibly best known for his books, **Birthright**[34] and **Alive for the First Time**,[35] unveiled the wonders of this complex word as seen in the book of Hosea. In this Old Testament prophetic book as well as throughout the Old Testament, the word **hesed** is often translated in a vast array of ways: mercy, lovingkindness, love, steadfast love. This points to the value of checking a variety of translations when reading the Bible. Any time we see a Biblical word translated in many different ways in various translations, it could be an indicator of a word for which we have no English equivalent.

Such is the case with **hesed**. Let's look at it in the book of Hosea. So, God told the prophet Hosea, a godly man of integrity, that God would give him a wife and that his marriage was going to serve as a metaphor in communicating to God's people. Now prophets were comfortable with metaphors because so much of what they spoke was poetic; so much was a picture of an important truth. But God was saying that

---

[34] David C. Needham, *Birthright: Christian*, Multnomah Publishers, 1979.
[35] David C. Needham, *Alive for the First Time*, Multnomah Books, 1995.

Hosea's marriage, in itself, was going to be a metaphor, an object lesson, so that God's people would truly see his love for them. Well, that could be cool. I'd sign up for that because surely the metaphor would be one of perfect love. Perfect two-way love.

But that was not the situation. God commanded Hosea to take Gomer as his wife and Gomer had a reputation. She was "a promiscuous woman" (Hosea 1:2) who, in her unfaithfulness to Hosea, was going to be a picture of Israel's unfaithfulness to God. And Hosea was told to continue to love Gomer, even in her unfaithfulness, as a picture of God's loyal love to Israel. They had three children and one was, evidently, not Hosea's. Hosea became a solo father as Gomer went back to her early life and as her life worsened beyond what she had previously known. God told Hosea to rescue his wife from slavery and Hosea had to actually pay for her freedom before he brought her back home, as his wife. Still.

What a stunning picture of what would later be found in Jesus as he came to earth. In the midst of humanity's rebellion to the loyal love of God, God would provide a way. He would provide healing for humankind's relationship with him through the redemptive blood of Jesus. Though God created us and we were his, he would buy us out of slavery to restore us to himself, our Creator and our Redeemer.

For I desire steadfast love and not sacrifice,
the knowledge of God rather than burnt offerings.
Hosea 6:6 ESV

Hesed is an enduring love, a steadfast love. Maybe that's why it is a word that is primarily used for God's love for humanity rather than for human love. It is love in the context of a covenant, a commitment. This word is used approximately 248 times in the Old Testament. It is the word used in Hosea 4:1, 6:6, 10:12, and 12:6. It is a love that will not let us go. We belong to God, our Creator and our Redeemer. His love is enduring through thick and thin. And what I remember most from Mr. Needham's teaching long ago in that Bible College course is this phrase – "***hesed*** is a two-way street". ***Hesed,*** in the context of covenant and faithfulness, is expected from both parties. Even though, throughout Scripture, we see God's people fail in their part of the covenant, God continues to do his part. Throughout history he has and now he does. Still.

Another Old Testament word: ahab

There are other Hebrew words that are often translated "love" in our English Bibles and one is **ahab** or **aheb**. (As a side note, the word is not linked to wicked King Ahab whose name relates to the word "brother". This word, **ahab**, is better pronounced **achab** as in Bach.) Used approximately 200 times, this word for love is similar to the way we use "love" in English; it is an all-round, multi-purpose word. It is most often used for human love – love for good things, people and ideas as well as love for evil things, people, and ideas. In Genesis 24:67[36] this is the word used for Isaac's love for his wife, Rebekah. It is used for human love for an object or an idea such as the love of wisdom in Prov-

---

[36] "Isaac brought her into the tent of his mother Sarah, and he married Rebekah. So she became his wife, and he loved her; and Isaac was comforted after his mother's death." Genesis 24:67.

erbs 4:6.[37] It is the word for the love of folly or for the love of sin in Proverbs 17:19.[38] In fact, **ahab** is often used when describing a strong appetite for food, drink, sleep and objects to possess.

This word is only used for God's love approximately 27 times. When **ahab** occurs in the book of Hosea it is most often in the context of Gomer's sinful love and lovers. Throughout its Old Testament usage, **ahab** shows a strong emotional attachment to something that can often be quite negative.

I am profoundly struck by the contrast of these two Hebrew words, **hesed** and **ahab**. When compared to **ahab**, the power and commitment and complete goodness of **hesed** is quite obvious. Therefore, it makes complete sense that it is used to describe the love of God. **Hesed** is love on a whole other level. It's a mind-blowing, gobsmacking love that just won't let go. Maybe it's time that we adopt the term into our English vocabulary. Just last night, to a living room filled with guests, I referred to the **hesed** of God and a couple of them uttered "oooooohs" in deep appreciation for the fullness of the meaning of that little word. So, practice your guttural "kh" sound and begin to regularly talk about the **hesed** of God. For a discussion on its pronunciation and more of its nuanced meaning, I refer you to The Bible Project podcast on loyal love.[39] Aren't you grateful for the **hesed** of God? I most certainly am. In fact, I'm going to pause right now and thank him. Maybe you could join me.

---

[37] "Do not forsake wisdom, and she will protect you; love her, and she will watch over you." Proverbs 4:6.
[38] "Whoever loves a quarrel loves sin; whoever builds a high gate invites destruction." Proverbs 17:19.
[39] The Bible Project, https://bibleproject.com/podcast/series/character-of-god. Used by permission.

One of many Greek words: agape

...our model is the Jesus, not only of Calvary,
but of the workshop, the roads, the crowds, the clamorous demands
and surly oppositions, the lack of all peace and privacy, the interruptions.
For this, so strangely unlike anything we can attribute to the divine life in itself
is apparently not only like, but is, the Divine life operating under human conditions."

C.S. Lewis[40]

Various forms of the word "love" are used 46 times in the little letter of 1 John. The Greek word used most often for God's love is **agape** and it appears frequently in this letter, both as a noun and as a verb, **agapao**. Other Greek words that are translated "love" tend to be used more for various types of human love. **Agapao** is a love that cares, a love that chooses to be concerned with the wellbeing of the other. It is a love that is unconditional. It is not a response to someone who is lovely but, rather, a choice to seek good for another regardless of their level of loveliness. We read in 1 John 4:8 that God IS love. Love is always his character and love is always his action. In fact, God has always been love. When Jesus was praying to the Father, he said, "... you loved me before the foundation of the world" (John 17:24 ESV). Love is part of what defines God's attitude toward himself and toward humanity.

This idea of a loving God was, and still is, a foreign concept to most people across the globe. If, as you've read this chapter, you've felt

[40] C.S. Lewis, *The Four Loves*, Harcourt, Inc., 1960, 1991 edition, p. 6. © copyright CS Lewis Pte Ltd 1960. Used by permission.

like maybe I've been over-selling the love of God, you might have good reason. I believe that it is fair to say that only in Christianity do we find a God who is described as loving. The gods of the Ancient Near East were anything but loving; words like self-absorbed, vengeful, immoral, unpredictable, and difficult to please come to mind. Not loving. Even today, when we examine world religions, we see gods who are very much the same as the ancient gods.

My husband and I lived in Saudi Arabia for about five years in the 2010s. It was a fascinating and not-always-pleasant experience. What I cherished the most was developing friendships with people who had never encountered the God of the Bible. Their view of God was a very distant and unpredictable power with whom one could never be sure of their standing. No matter the number of prayers said in a day, regardless of the number of trips to a mosque, no one was sure that they would be "in" or "out" with God. And certainly, my friends were baffled by the idea of having a personal relationship with God, of sitting in silence with God and having nothing to prove. This love of God is no fairy tale. It is **agape**. 1 John 4:9[41] says that God's love was "made manifest" or "revealed" or "shown" to us. In many ways, we need to "see" love to believe it.

Love is and love does

God's love, which has been very real throughout his relationship with humanity, has been revealed to us in Jesus. Jesus came to earth as Love incarnate. Jesus is Love that we can see and Love that we can observe in action. Love IS and love DOES.

---

[41] "In this the love of God was made manifest among us, that God sent his only Son into the world, so that we might live through him." 1 John 4:9 ESV.

Here's more of 1 John 4 in its context. Notice the noun, the idea of love, and notice the verb, the action of love. Each are vital aspects of God's love and of our love that can become more and more like God's love.

---

*Dear friends, let us **love** one another, for **love** comes from God.*
*Everyone who **loves** has been born of God and knows God.*
*Whoever does not **love** does not know God, because God is **love**.*
*This is how God showed his **love** among us:*
He sent his one and only Son into the world that we might live through him.
*This is **love**: not that we **loved** God, but that he **loved** us*
and sent his Son as an atoning sacrifice for our sins.
*Dear friends, since God so **loved** us, we also ought to **love** one another.*
*No one has ever seen God; but if we **love** one another,*
*God lives in us and his **love** is made complete in us.*
*And so we know and rely on the **love** God has for us. God is **love**.*
*Whoever lives in **love** lives in God, and God in them.*
*This is how **love** is made complete among us so that we will have confidence*
*on the day of judgment: In this world we are like Jesus. There is no fear in **love**.*
*But perfect **love** drives out fear, because fear has to do with punishment.*
*The one who fears is not made perfect in **love**.*
*We **love** because he first **loved** us. Whoever claims to **love***
God yet hates a brother or sister is a liar.
*For whoever does not **love** their brother and sister, whom they have seen,*
*cannot **love** God, whom they have not seen.*
And he has given us this command:
*Anyone who **loves** God must also **love** their brother and sister.*

1 John 4:7-12;16-21, emphasis added

Unshakeable!

> *For I am convinced that neither death nor life,*
> *neither angels nor demons, neither the present nor the future,*
> *nor any powers, neither height nor depth, nor anything else in all creation,*
> *will be able to separate us from the love of God*
> *that is in Christ Jesus our Lord.*
> **Romans 8:38-39**

There are two major reasons that God's love for me is unshakeable. One has to do with me and the other has to do with God. If God's love depended upon me, it would be a very shaky thing. I am fickle and flaky and finicky. I can only imagine the disastrous insecurity I would know if my relationship with God depended upon me. As we've already discussed, hallelujah that it does not depend upon me. God's love does not depend upon you. Only Jesus. Our security in our relationship with God rests on him, alone. God does not remove his love for us, even when our actions and thoughts and attitudes are quite unlovely.

I am reminded of a question I was recently asked by a young adult leader in our church. It was a terrific question – "Cheap grace or salvation by works? Which is it?" My answer was, "Neither! Costly grace, very costly grace." As we discussed in the chapters on mercy and grace, God's love for humankind costs humans nothing. But that absolutely does not mean that God's love is cheap. It could never be called cheap because it cost God everything. It is incredibly costly grace.

Secondly, God's love is unshakeable because God is unshakeable. Hebrews 13:8 states this fact: "Jesus Christ is the same yesterday and today and forever." Three of the many words that can never be used to describe God are: fickle, flaky and finicky. God does not change. James 1:17[42] says that God does not change like shifting shadows. That's an unchanging fact. I so appreciate these lyrics from a much-loved song by Ben Fielding and Dean Ussher.

Unchanging One
You who was and is to come
Your promise sure
You will not let go
There is hope in the promise of the cross
You gave everything to save the world You love
And this hope is an anchor for my soul
Our God will stand Unshakeable[43]

Symbols of love

On my first Mother's Day as a mother, our daughter was a little over eight months old. By this time, I had been in my new role long enough to feel utterly inadequate. And to top it off, my teeth were in braces so I looked much too young to be a parent; I looked like I'd qualify to be her babysitter. My husband wanted to honour me that day so, as I sat in a rocker on my parents' deck by the lake on that lovely, Alaskan,

---

[42] "Every good and perfect gift is from above, coming down from the Father of the heavenly lights, who does not change like shifting shadows," James 1:17.
[43] *Anchor*, Words and Music by Ben Fielding & Dean Ussher, © 2012 Hillsong Music Publishing. Used by permission.

Spring day, I soaked up the moment when Jim "helped" our daughter, Jeri, hand me my Mother's Day gift. My first gift as a mom. Wow! With delight, I tore into what would, I was sure, be absolutely stunning.

It was not. It was an electric toothbrush.

My ever-practical husband knew that this gift would be a great accompaniment to my braces. As I looked at the gift on my lap, I wondered how best to respond. And as I lifted my gaze upward, my eyes caught the eyes of my own mother. Those eyes said, strongly and clearly, "He loves you, Sharon. He really, really loves you. Just smile and say how much you love it." I did.

Love is practical, sometimes. Love sees a need and decides to respond. That toothbrush became a symbol to me of my husband's very practical love. When he vacuums the house before company arrives, he is saying, "I love you". When he turns his dream fountain project into a fountain with multiple waterfalls (my dream: to live by a waterfall) he is saying "I love you". The sound of the waterfall outside our bedroom window serves as a constant reminder of my husband's sacrificial and tangible love. When I sneak away from a noisy household to sit by that lovely waterfall, I am reminded that I am loved.

On Valentine's Day 1994, I baked Jim a dozen long-stemmed cookies. Yes, you read that right. It was something that I'd seen advertised at a shop and, being a do-it-yourselfer, I figured I'd spend time instead of money. So, I produced some pretty terrific oatmeal raisin cookies, each one wrapped in red cellophane with a little red bow, on the end of long floral stems with lovely artificial greenery, resting in appropriate florist's paper all tucked inside a long, white, long-stemmed-roses box, which was wrapped in a gorgeous red ribbon. I must admit that I was rather pleased with myself. The presentation was lovely; Jim thought the cookies were lovely. I'm not sure that he noticed the presentation, actually. I could have saved a lot of time and money and just baked him a batch of cookies. Yet, we were each happy with the results in different ways. But then, as the evening progressed, it became apparent to me that my husband had forgotten that it was Valentine's Day. Now, in the USA, to forget Valentine's Day is an offence of criminal proportions. No loving husband forgets Valentine's Day. So, my position on the unhappiness scale was moving up by the minute.

And then, as the kids were all successfully asleep and as I was getting ready to retire to my pity party, Jim walked into our bedroom with a little box. It was one of those boxes that only comes from one place: a jewellery store. And the size of this particular box indicated that it could only contain one thing: a ring. Before opening anything, we both had a good laugh. No matter what was inside the box, the existence of that box meant that my husband who (at that season in his life) was very averse to shopping, not only shopped but shopped in a jewellery store. Even before I opened the box, I felt so loved. And then, when I finally opened the box, I found a lovely opal ring. My birthstone. It was stunning. I cried. A lot. My husband loved me so much that he would shop. He would shop in a type of store that didn't sell nuts and bolts and tools. And he would choose a ring that he knew I would love. Forget practical! That ring became a symbol of my husband's sacrificial and romantic love.

Fast track to the year 2000. We were building (I use the term "we" loosely because it was mainly Jim) our dream log home in Colorado. The Alaskan way to build a house is to move in before there is running water, interior walls… any niceties… and then build as you live there. Our area of Colorado, just outside of Denver, had stricter regulations so we couldn't move in until all of the basics were done. But finishing touches, like flooring, weren't yet completed. One morning, after showering, I realised that my opal was no longer in my ring. I needed to head right out the door to my job at church, but we (I use the term "we" loosely, again, because it was mainly just me) went into a bit of a panic as we retraced my steps of the morning. My father had come down from Alaska to help Jim finish the house, so while the empty ring sat on my dresser and while I was at work, Jim and Dad took the plumbing apart on the shower and the sink. No opal was to be found. That evening we searched some more. Nothing. Slowly, it began to sink in that the opal was gone.

Three days later, I did something I rarely do. I came home in the middle of the day to fix lunch for Jim and Dad. And before I headed back out, I did something I never do. As I sat in one of our wing back chairs in the living room, I put my elbows on my knees and rested my chin in my hands. I think I was sulking. And then. Then my eyes fell on the huge rust-coloured braided rug/carpet. A rug on an unfinished floor. A rug in a construction zone. Because it was a work zone, I had vacuumed that rug and the surrounding floor at least twice a day for weeks. And on that rug, my eyes caught a small oval. It was not shiny in any way. There was no reason to notice it. But I was seeing the back side of my opal.

As I type, I'm looking at that opal on the ring finger on my right hand. A place that has always been its home. That ring is now a symbol of being twice loved – once by my dear husband and once by my dear God! God kept that opal safe and out of the vacuum for three days and he brought me home to cook lunch so that I could find it. How kind of God to love me, not just practically but just because. Just because he is love. It was a hug from heaven.

Do you feel it – the struggle to adequately describe the love of God? Do you know it – the love of God, personally? You didn't get in on a group rate. His love is for you. And you. And you. Individually, yet inclusively.

The Love of God (Verse 3)
Could we with ink the ocean fill,
and were the skies of parchment made,
Were every stalk on earth a quill,
and everyone a scribe by trade,
To write the love of God above,
would drain the ocean dry.
Nor could the scroll contain the whole,
though stretched from sky to sky.

Frederick M. Lehman[44]

---

[44] Frederick M. Lehman, The Love of God, 1923, Public Domain.

For Reflection

1. Find a version of **The Love of God,** which is mentioned above and give it a careful listen. I would recommend Mercy Me's recording of it, but there are many versions, including the classic with George Beverly Shea. Meditate on the words, picturing every stalk on earth being a quill pen and the entire sky being filled and overflowing with words of God's love.

2. Read 1 Corinthians 13, substituting the word "love" with the name "God". Spend some time thanking God for the specifics of his love. Now, read the chapter again, substituting the word "love" with your name. Journal about the accuracy of that description for you. Wherever you find a good match, thank God for his work in you. Wherever you find some lack, talk with God about your need.

3. Make a list of the "hugs from heaven" that you have received in the past two weeks. This might take some effort to find the hugs that you have missed. Share your list with someone. How very kind of God to verb-love us. We need hugs in order to truly see the reality of God's love.

4. God's love is not "safe", but it is good. Maybe it's the risk involved in love that brings our hesitancy. Contemplate this section from **The Four Loves** by C.S. Lewis.[45]

To love at all is to be vulnerable. Love anything, and your heart will certainly be wrung and possibly be broken. If you want to make sure of keeping it intact, you must give your heart to no one, not even to an animal. Wrap it carefully round with hobbies and little luxuries; avoid all entanglements; lock it up safe in the casket or coffin of your selfishness. But in that casket – safe, dark, motionless, airless – it will change. It will not be broken; it will become unbreakable, impenetrable, irredeemable. The alternative to tragedy, or at least to the risk of tragedy, is damnation. The only place outside Heaven where you can be perfectly safe from all the dangers and perturbations of love is Hell.

7

GOD IS FAITHFUL

> *Because of the Lord's great love*
> *we are not consumed,*
> *for his compassions never fail.*
> *They are new every morning;*
> *great is your faithfulness.*

Lamentations 3:22-23

This is a fitting verse to begin our next focus, as it links some thoughts on God's great and loyal love, **hesed,** with related thoughts found in this word "faithful". The idea conveyed with this Hebrew word is one of complete integrity, dependability, consistency. When used with **hesed**, it reinforces the loyal, covenantal love of God for humanity by reminding us that this loyal love is steadfast and consistently good. In the midst of his lament, Jeremiah reminds himself that the only reason the unfaithful people of God are not consumed is that, even while they are unfaithful, God remains faithful. What a beautiful picture is painted across the sky, here. In a setting that deserves destruction, it is a new morning. God's compassions never fail. They never run empty. With every sunrise, it's as though God offers a new dose of compassion. That is the beauty of God's faithfulness. He is fully trustworthy.

Remember back to the various times we've discussed Exodus 34:6. "Faithful" is the last word of the five characteristics of God, which are mentioned in the verse. Let's quickly revisit the context. God describes himself with these terms immediately after the Hebrew people began to enter into a covenant with Almighty God and epically failed. As Moses was back up on Mt. Sinai, the people he led did the unthinkable. They gathered all of their valuable gold objects, melted them down and forged a calf made of that gold. What a shocking picture of unfaithfulness – bowing in worship before an object they had just made. They had the audacity to transfer their loyalty from the worship of The One who created them to the worship of some THING they created. Even if their intention was to create a representation of the one, true God, they were settling for an image rather than God, himself. Tragic. Silly, even. And it's all too common in our modern-day forms of idolatry where we worship creation instead of appreciating and caring for creation, allowing it to point us to the Creator. When we put anyone or anything in a place of value that is reserved for our Most High God, we are sliding toward idolatry.

Together, the Hebrew and the Greek word clusters around this word "faithful" occur in the Bible more than 1500 times. The adjective can be translated to faithful, trustworthy, believable; the noun forms can be translated to faith, trust, belief; and the verb forms can be translated to have faith in, trust in, believe in. These are words with which "people of faith" are very familiar. Maybe, sometimes, we are overly familiar with these terms and need to become re-acquainted.

As Christians, our faith in God is not a blind leap off of a cliff into something that is unseen. We are actually able to be full of faith because God is full of faith-fulness. We see his faithfulness throughout Scripture. We see his faithfulness in the rhythm of the sunrise and sunset. We see his faithfulness in our lives. We might not see or understand where we are headed, but our faith is not in where we are headed. Our faith is in the God who knows tomorrow and has proven himself faithful.

I once heard the contrast of paddling a canoe with rowing a row boat. I've been in many canoes in my day and I've been in a few rowboats (not the racing, crew-team style). When you're alone in a canoe with one paddle, where do you sit? In the back or, more appropriately, the stern. When you're paddling that canoe, you are facing forward, anticipating every snag in the river, every set of rapids and you are using your best J stroke in order to avoid having the bow, or front of the canoe, swing from left to right and back. You are in control of the river or lake. Or at least you feel like you are! The key to success in a canoe is alert anticipation.

When you are alone in a simple rowboat, with two oars that are usually in oar locks, where do you sit? In the middle, facing backward. You don't know what is ahead of you because you can't see it. So, you fix your eyes on a spot on the shore that you are leaving and as you stay steadily in line with that spot you can stay on course without constantly checking over your shoulder. You are in control of the rowboat, but you cannot anticipate and be alert to what is ahead. The key to success in a rowboat is fixing your sight on the right object.

Do you get my point? Faith is not about climbing into a canoe and trying to be the master of your journey. Faith is about sitting in a rowboat, moving forward with confidence because you are fixing your eyes on

God's faithfulness in the past. We can trust God with our tomorrows because he has been faithful in our yesterdays. So, let's review God's faithfulness in history's yesterdays.

Looking back

Firstly, we are reminded of the promise God made in his covenant with his people. It was very clear what they were to do and what he would do.

---

*It was not because you were more in number than any other people that the Lord set his love on you and chose you, for you were the fewest of all peoples, but it is because the Lord loves you and is keeping the oath that he swore to your fathers, that the Lord has brought you out with a mighty hand and redeemed you from the house of slavery, from the hand of Pharaoh king of Egypt. Know therefore that the Lord your God is God, the **<u>faithful God</u>** who keeps covenant and steadfast love with those who love him and keep his commandments, to a thousand generations, and repays to their face those who hate him, by destroying them. He will not be slack with one who hates him. He will repay him to his face. You shall therefore be careful to do the commandment and the statutes and the rules that I command you today. And because you listen to these rules and keep and do them, the Lord your God will keep with you the covenant and the steadfast love that he swore to your fathers. He will love you, bless you, and multiply you.*

Deuteronomy 7:7-13a ESV, emphasis added

Though we see the reality that God was consistently and unshakably faithful to his promises, it is also true that his people were consistent in their unfaithfulness. Yet, because of God's great mercy, he often delayed giving them what they deserved. In Judges 2:10 we read that "another generation grew up who knew neither the Lord nor what he had done for Israel". Timothy Keller explains this further:

The word "knew" probably does not mean that they did not know about the Exodus, the Red Sea, the crossing of the Jordan, and the walls of Jericho falling, but rather that the saving acts of God were no longer precious or central to them. They had not learned to revere and rejoice in what God had done. In other words, they had forgotten the "gospel" that they were saved from slavery in Egypt and brought into the promised land by the gracious, mighty acts of God. Put simply, they forgot.
Timothy Keller[46]

So, these people KNEW OF God but did not KNOW him. These people who had a rich history of God's character on display for them simply forgot the reality of their salvation. This is not a human tendency that is limited to the Old Testament. In John:39-40 Jesus calls out the Jewish leaders on the very same problem. "You study the Scriptures diligently because you think that in them you have eternal life. These are the very Scriptures that testify about me, yet you refuse to come to me to have life". Lest we begin the arrogant tsk-tsk-ing at generations of old, with great haste let us acknowledge that we are no different today. We are "these people"! This is our pattern as individuals and as groups of individuals. So easily we settle for knowing OF God without truly knowing him. And yet... God is faithful.

Generation after generation sought God when in a season of distress

---

[46] Timothy Keller, *God's Word For Your Judges For You*, The Good Book Company, Purcellville, VA, 2017, p. 30. Used by permission of The Good Book Company.

and quickly forgot God when in a season of ease. Psalm 78 records this pattern. I'll highlight just a few verses from this chapter.

> *...they did not keep God's covenant*
> *and refused to live by his law.*
> *They forgot what he had done,*
> *the wonders he had shown them.*
> *How often they rebelled against him in the wilderness*
> *and grieved him in the wasteland!*
> *Again and again they put God to the test;*
> *they vexed the Holy One of Israel.*
> *They did not remember his power*
> *the day he redeemed them from the oppressor,*
>
> *But they put God to the test and rebelled against the Most High;*
> *they did not keep his statutes.*
> *Like their ancestors they were disloyal and faithless,*
> *as unreliable as a faulty bow.*
>
> **Psalm 78:10-11; 40-42; 56-57**

And yet... God is faithful.

> *I have a message from God in my heart*
> *concerning the sinfulness of the wicked:*
> *There is no fear of God*
> *before their eyes.*
> *In their own eyes they flatter themselves*
> *too much to detect or hate their sin.*
> *The words of their mouths are wicked and deceitful;*

> *they fail to act wisely or do good.*
> *Even on their beds they plot evil;*
> *they commit themselves to a sinful course*
> *and do not reject what is wrong.*
> *Your love, Lord, reaches to the heavens,*
> *your **faithfulness** to the skies.*
> *Your righteousness is like the highest mountains,*
> *your justice like the great deep.*
> *You, Lord, preserve both people and animals.*
> *How priceless is your unfailing love, O God!*
> *People take refuge in the shadow of your wings.*
>
> **Psalm 36:1-7, emphasis added**

Faithful in forgiving

Not too long after our son, Joey, surrendered his young life to Jesus, he was very disturbed by his behaviour in the events of the day. It took me back to my own restless nights, between ages almost-five and six, when I doubted that God really had redeemed me. My sin caused me to doubt that I truly belonged to God and Joey's struggle was similar. That night, long after I thought the children were asleep and I had climbed into bed, Joey arrived at my bedside. He had apologised to every offended person he could think of. He had apologised to God. And yet the struggle was real. "How could God love me?" he asked in his six-year-old way. "I don't feel very forgiven."

So, I asked Joey to tiptoe into the bedroom he shared with Brad and to retrieve the globe off of their dresser. He returned and climbed up on my bed with the globe. I asked him to pick a spot on the earth. He stuck his finger on a place and held it there. So, I instructed him to move his finger up the globe in a straight line and to keep moving it slowly up. As he did so, I asked what direction he was going. He said, "North!" I affirmed that truth and told him to keep moving his finger and let me know when his finger started moving south. He joyously did. And we kept that movement going, first north and then south and then north, again. He thought that was cool.

Then I asked him to pick another spot on the globe and instructed him to start moving his finger east. He eagerly did so. And I asked him to let me know when his finger started moving west. He kept slowly moving his finger - east, east, east, ... more east ... never west. It never reached a point where it switched to west! Then we looked up the following verse.

---

*...as far as the east is from the west,
so far has he removed our transgressions from us.*
Psalm 103:12

Now, imagine God saying, "Oh, that's so cool! How lucky for us all that I chose to say east/west instead of north/south." I'm chuckling just thinking about that. No, that's not how God would respond. There's nothing accidental with, or surprising to, God! God, the all-knowing and all-wise God, chose to say that our sins are removed as far as the east is from the west. North Pole to South Pole is a pretty astounding distance but east to west? Well, that's beyond beyond!

How very kind of God to reassure my son that the memory of that sin AND the access to that memory are removed so very far that they can't be retrieved! Joey slept well that night. He slept in the peace of forgiveness.

Shame and guilt

What about when we don't sleep in the peace of forgiveness? What about when you just can't seem to shake the sorrow you feel about something you did yesterday or many yesterdays ago? Let's talk a bit about the difference between shame and guilt.

As a mother, I learned to love guilt. Okay. Maybe I'm overstating that to get your attention, but allow me to explain. When one of my children was disobedient, I did not want to shame them into conformity. I did not want to berate them and cut their fragile ego into pieces. I wanted them to feel godly sorrow that leads to repentance as in 2 Corinthians 7:10.[47] And so they would have consequences.

Sometimes, however, because of my own unreasonable emotions, they went to their room and didn't think about their sin at all. This has been one of the toughest parenting concepts for me to learn and I'm pretty certain I still haven't mastered it – when we react rather than respond, we weaken the potential impact of the consequence our child is facing. On the days that my own emotions were out of control, when my anger was expressed in unhealthy ways, my children just thought about their mean and unreasonable mother.

But on a good day, a day the Holy Spirit was in control of my own

[47] "Godly sorrow brings repentance that leads to salvation and leaves no regret, but worldly sorrow brings death." 2 Corinthians 7:10.

heart and actions, they had no distractions and could face their sin. And then they felt sorrow over that sin. And that sorrow led them to repent and seek forgiveness from me or from a sibling and to most definitely seek forgiveness from God.

You see, when we feel any level of guilt and bring it to God, God says, "I've been waiting for you. Yes, you are guilty; you are guilty, indeed. I totally forgive you." God is faithful to forgive.

---

*If we confess our sins, he is faithful and just
and will forgive us our sins and
purify us from all unrighteousness.*
1 John 1:9

So, when we still feel angst over that sin that we already confessed, what we are feeling is not sorrow over unconfessed sin. It is, most likely, shame. Now God never shames us. Throughout Scripture, you never see God wagging his finger at someone, saying, "Shame on you." Parents might, regrettably, do that to their children. A "friend" might do that to us. Satan does it. Regularly. But that response is not consistent with God's character.

If this is striking a chord for you, I encourage you to talk further with a pastor or a godly counsellor or psychologist. God longs to free you from shame. David speaks about this, from personal experience:

> *I sought the Lord, and he answered me;*
> *he delivered me from all my fears.*
> *Those who look to him are radiant;*
> *their faces are never covered with shame.*
> *This poor man called, and the Lord heard him;*
> *he saved him out of all his troubles.*
>
> **Psalm 34:4-6 ESV**

The simplest way I can guide you to what to do in these situations is a bit corny, but it's memorable: "G G to G" and "S S to S". If you are guilty, quit trying to pretend that you are not. Admit your sin to the one you hurt. Admit your sin to God. Our very trustworthy God is faithful to forgive you. **<u>Give the Guilt to God</u>** – "G G to G".

And if you are shaming yourself or if you are hearing someone's voice inside your head saying, "Shame on you!" – **<u>Send the Shame to Satan</u>** – "S S to S". Send it to the pit of hell. It doesn't belong to you. I'm remembering, as I write, some really immature things I've done as an adult, those times when I should have known better but I still blew it. I am embarrassed by my reaction in those moments. The reason I want to hang my head and hide with the memory is because what I'm feeling is shame. And I'm trapped in those memories because God forgave me but I still don't like to remember what I did. Are you living in some kind of shame? Ask God to free you from that shame. Ask him to free you from any and all shame, minute or massive. Just as David did, cry out to God and the Lord will hear you and rescue you.

Preamble to The Ten Commandments

I'm always amazed when I stop for a moment and realise that, though we often think of the Old Testament as a collection of laws, it actually took 70 chapters, one and a half books of the Bible, all of Genesis and half of Exodus, for God to begin to give specific laws that were recorded. That means that it took the generations through Adam and Eve, Cain and Abel, Enoch, Methuselah, Noah, Abraham, Isaac, and Jacob and then all of the way to the later years of the life of Moses before God gave his people the Law. Why then? They had just become a new nation. Nations are established and their distinctions become clear through laws and policies and procedures. Their laws are part of what set Israel apart from their neighbours.

Do you want to see another amazing element? Check out verse 2 of Exodus 20. That's the chapter where we find what we call The Ten Commandments. After waiting so many generations, God still delayed spelling out the laws for a moment longer in order to remind his people of the foundation of the laws. The rock-solid foundation was God's commitment to them. So, he began the laws with this reminder of his loyal love and faithfulness, "I am the Lord your God, who brought you out of Egypt, out of the land of slavery." A covenant is a reciprocal relationship and God was about to tell this new nation the ten major laws that they were required to uphold in that covenant relationship.

The faithfulness of God is magnified when we put it in the context of God's fore-knowledge. He knew they would fail miserably; he knew that they would be unfaithful in the very near future when they gathered their gold treasures in order to create an idol for their corporate worship – a completely false, unreal, fake-news god. God knew that he would be faithful, still. It's as though faithfulness is the ground where all of God's other attributes meet. He will always be who he is. Even though. Yet. Still. He will.

Rocks

One of the best pictures of faithfulness is a rock. In general terms a rock is stable, unchanging and unmovable. Rain, snow, gales, quakes – the rock remains. Though imperfect, as are all illustrations, a rock is a picture of God that we see repeated throughout the Psalms and in many other passages of Scripture. In 2 Samuel 23:3[48] God is called "the Rock of Israel". We see this again in Isaiah 30:29.[49] 1 Samuel 2:2[50] shows us that even when the illustration fails, when a rock does roll in life, God is a rock that is not like any other rock.

Turn your ear to me,
come quickly to my rescue;
be my rock of refuge,
a strong fortress to save me.
Since you are my rock and my fortress,
for the sake of your name lead and guide me.

Psalm 31:2-3

---

[48] "The God of Israel spoke, the Rock of Israel said to me: 'When one rules over people in righteousness, when he rules in the fear of God,'" 2 Samuel 23:3.
[49] "And you will sing as on the night you celebrate a holy festival; your hearts will rejoice as when people playing pipes go up to the mountain of the Lord, to the Rock of Israel." Isaiah 30:29.
[50] "There is no one holy like the Lord; there is no one besides you; there is no Rock like our God." 1 Samuel 2:2.

What an interesting thought! The Psalmist says to God, in my paraphrase, "Since you are my rock, for the sake of your character, be a rock for me." I believe the Psalmist truly understood the faithfulness of God – that God must be who he is. Always.

God, being who He is, cannot cease to be what He is,
and being what He is, He cannot act out of character with Himself.
He is at once faithful and immutable,
so all His words and acts must be and must remain faithful.
Men become unfaithful out of desire, fear, loss of interest,
or because of some strong influence from without.
Obviously none of these forces can affect God in any way.
He is His own reason for all He is and does.

A.W. Tozer[51]

A bit about belief

If you declare with your mouth, "Jesus is Lord,"
*and **believe** in your heart that God raised him from the dead,*
you will be saved.
*For it is with your heart that you **believe** and are justified,*
*and it is with your mouth that you profess your **faith** and are saved.*

Romans 10:9-10, emphasis added

---

[51] A.W. Tozer, The Knowledge of the Holy, Harper & Row, 1961, 1975 edition, p. 85.

So now we land on this topic of belief. After establishing the complete trustworthiness of God, belief might not seem to be quite the leap we once thought it to be. The risk is not so much in the leap but, rather, in the place that leap takes us.

When I was about 6 years old, I believed I could fly. Now, I was careful to tell my parents that I wasn't so ridiculous that I thought I could fly very far and I certainly didn't even want to fly very high. But I was absolutely certain that I could fly for a short while. I was convinced that after I took air, I hung there, suspended in space, for a short moment. I was so certain of this that I got rather bruised when I hit the blinds on the window of my parents' bedroom after "taking flight" from their bed. My nose and arms were a bit bruised. My ego was majorly bruised.

The amount of faith I had was not in question. I had full faith in my ability to fly. My faith was larger than my small body, to be sure! But it was a misplaced faith. Seriously misplaced.

Belief is only as good as what we believe IN! What a relief it is to learn that our salvation does not depend upon the amount of faith or belief we have. Two verses that come to mind are terrific verses of comfort in this matter. In Matthew 17:20[52] Jesus tells us, metaphorically, that amazing things can happen with faith the size of a mustard seed.

Have you seen a mustard seed? It's about 1-2 mm in diameter. It's rather unimpressive and is one of the smallest seeds on the planet. It was the smallest seed one would plant in New Testament times and was a rapid

---

[52] "He replied, 'Because you have so little faith. Truly I tell you, if you have faith as small as a mustard seed, you can say to this mountain, 'Move from here to there,' and it will move. Nothing will be impossible for you.'" Matthew 17:20.

grower, even in parched conditions. This concept would have been familiar to the audience hearing Jesus that day. Amazingly, in a matter of a few years, a mustard seed can grow into a tree that is 20 to 30 feet tall. And it can become as wide as it is tall. Such a massive tree from such a small beginning. Refreshing thought? Certainly. The size of the seed has absolutely no bearing on the size of the result. Hallelujah!

In Mark 9, a man brings his son through the vast crowds in order to have Jesus heal the boy. In verse 24 of Mark 9, the man so very honestly says to Jesus, "I do believe; help me overcome my unbelief." What attractive honesty. And what a comforting response we see in Jesus. Immediately, Jesus healed the boy. The healing was not dependent upon the amount of faith this father held. The point is that this father's faith, no matter how feeble, was appropriately placed in Jesus.

The faith-hope-joy link

The first overseas living adventure that Jim and I began in 2006 was in Port Harcourt, Nigeria. I do believe that I left part of my heart in that country. Our time there was not without its struggles. But we saw, on a daily basis, that in Nigeria, struggles lived right alongside faith, hope and joy. I can still remember the local dialect lyrics for a simple chorus taught to me by a young woman named Gloria. It was sung with vibrancy and joy. And dancing. Always dancing. The English is simple: Things are getting better. Things are getting better. When God is on the throne, things are getting better. Things are getting better. Things are getting better.

That sums up the faith of Nigerian Christians – God is faithful so definitely things are getting better. God's faithfulness produced a hope and a joy that was contagious. I can hear that boisterous joy and see the exuberant dancing as I write.

A heart at rest

> *For it is by grace you have been saved, through **faith**—*
> *and this is not from yourselves, it is the gift of God—*
> *not by works, so that no one can boast.*
>
> **Ephesians 2:8-9, emphasis added**

Yes, our salvation requires faith. Simple faith. Whatever faith we have. Because we are saved, not by our works, this salvation is not from ourselves. It is a gift. What a phenomenal gift from our completely and consistently faithful God. I am grateful for the unshakeable, consistent, trustworthiness of God. My heart is at rest even as I type this.

> *Great is Thy faithfulness, O God, my Father;*
> *There is no shadow of turning with Thee.*
> *Summer and winter, and springtime and harvest,*
> *Sun, moon and stars in their courses above,*
> *Join with all nature in manifold witness*
> *To Thy great faithfulness, mercy and love.*
> *Great is Thy faithfulness!*
> *Great is Thy faithfulness!*
> *Morning by morning new mercies I see;*[53]

---

53 Thomas O. Chisholm and William M. Runyan, *Great Is Thy Faithfulness*, 1923, Public Domain.

For Reflection

1. In what ways have you worshipped something of your own creation? Are you still at risk of doing the same thing again? Talk with God about your propensity to forget him and follow after other gods of your own making. Surrender that problem to him, asking the Holy Spirit to help you live your life with only The One as your God!

2. Read all of Psalm 78, noting the contrast of human unfaithfulness and God's faithfulness.

3. Climb into a rowboat for a while, metaphorically speaking or "for reals". Look back at God's faithfulness in the past. Grab a journal or phone and record a list of examples of God's faithfulness to you. Meet with a friend and share your list. Encourage them to do the same. Spend some time "in the rowboat" with that friend as you praise God, together, for his faithfulness. Magnify the Lord with them.

4. What is in your life right now that seems to make it tough to trust God? I love the phrase "in the midst". Think about that little phrase. Right in the middle, right in the middle of something rough, God is there. You might not be able to trust a particular person or a particular system, but it is completely reasonable and safe to trust God. Talk with him about your situation. Ask him to help you with your unbelief!

PART TWO

His Purity

8
GOD IS HOLY

…thinness, hollow eyed gauntness, beards, sandals, long robes, stone cells, no sex, no jokes, hairshirts, cold baths, fasting, hours of prayer, rocky deserts, getting up at 4 a.m., clean fingernails, stained glass, and self-humiliation…

John White[54]

The above list may well be one of the most quoted sections from any of John White's writings. It is his own list of word associations when he considers the word "holiness". He acknowledges that the list is a bit strange and suggests that it is not to be read with frivolity but, rather, with weeping because of the tragic history of mankind's feeble attempts at the pursuit of holiness. (A basic explanation might be required for one term that may be unfamiliar – a hairshirt is a garment made from stiff cloth woven from horse or camel hair that was worn by religious zealots who wanted to punish themselves and wanted to demonstrate their sorrow for their sin.) It is quite obvious that this list doesn't begin to touch the true concept of holiness. Yet, what does it mean that God is holy? And what does holiness look like for us? Well, I certainly hope it's more than hairshirts.

I feel woefully inadequate to describe God's holiness because I am so

---

[54] John White, *The Fight: A Practical Handbook for Christian Living*, InterVarsity Press, 1976, p. 179. Used by permission.

very not. Not holy, that is. To think of God as holy requires much more than our language and behaviour provides. Think of the most perfect person you know – fiercely gentle, unmeasurably patient, unwaveringly committed, oozing only kindness... seemingly almost perfect. Now, to consider God's holiness we don't just take that description and polish it up a bit! God isn't merely better than the most perfect person you can imagine. A.W. Tozer wrestled with this idea, as he acknowledged that holiness refers to purity. But God's holiness is so much more than what God is not. God's holiness is not merely the absence of all that is wrong. It certainly is not simply being better than the most perfect human.

Holy is the way God is. To be holy He does not conform to a standard. He is the standard. He is absolutely holy with an infinite, incomprehensible fullness of purity that is incapable of being other than it is. Whatever is holy is healthy; evil is a moral sickness that must end ultimately in death.

A.W. Tozer[55]

Word origins

The origin of our English word, holy, helps us get closer to an understanding of its meaning. It comes from the German word **heilig**, meaning whole. That is why we can say, with A.W. Tozer in the above statement, that anything that is holy is healthy. It is complete and

---

[55] A.W. Tozer, *The Knowledge of the Holy*, Harper & Row, 1961, 1975 edition, pp. 112-113.

lacking nothing. Think of a completely healthy body. This requires imagination for every one of us because rarely is a body fully healthy. To be breathing means that we are decaying in some way. A completely healthy body would have every organ functioning at 100 percent capacity. There would be no nerves sending "ouch" messages to the brain of a completely healthy body.

If yours was a completely healthy body, and you were to focus on each individual part of your body from your toes to your hair, you would find no place that was even in need of relaxation. That thought is beyond my imagination, to be sure! In fact, no place would have pain or weakness. But a fully healthy body would not just be identified by what it wasn't. This perfectly healthy body would have massive energy and strength, enough strength to easily run an ultra-marathon. In the mountains. In a storm. Without shoes. (A shout-out to our son, Brad, an ultra-marathon runner – though I think he always wears shoes.) This would be a whole body. It's quite impossible this side of heaven.

The idea of wholeness is just one aspect of holiness. The most common words used for "holy" in both the Old Testament and the New Testament are concepts that mean set apart, otherness, sacred. The idea of being set apart is a fascinating study you might want to pursue in the Old Testament. You would find examples of things that are set apart for destruction as well as see things that are set apart for glory. So "holy" carries with it an idea of the distinction of being set apart for a special purpose.

> *"Who among the gods is like you, Lord?*
> *Who is like you—majestic in holiness,*
> *awesome in glory, working wonders?"*
>
> **Exodus 15:11**

When God is called holy, it not only means that he is "other" or different than humanity; it means that he is transcendently other. He is above all others. He is vastly above all of creation. He is the Supreme Other and the Only Other. We'll deal with that more in the chapter on God's sovereignty.

Repetitions

The poetic nature of Hebraic writing means that words are often repeated for emphasis. When we see patterns repeated, when we see phrases repeated, when we see words repeated – we should pay attention because it is intentional. For instance, names are often repeated for emphasis and to communicate intimacy in both the Old and New Testaments. Examples include: Absalom, Absalom; Simon, Simon; My God, My God; Saul, Saul.

When Jim and I lived in Indonesia, I studied Bahasa Indonesia (meaning "the language of Indonesia"). It is a relatively simple language to utilise because it is a contrived language, modelled after Malay and designed to unify the peoples on the hundreds of islands that became gathered into a nation called Indonesia. When we arrived at our new home on the island of Borneo, I quickly learned that most

Indonesians are trilingual, at their minimum. They speak their local language or languages, they speak Bahasa Indonesia, and they speak English. (I am proud to declare that, after many decades of labour, I am now becoming "bilingual", myself; I speak US American English and Aussie English.)

Though there are multiple layers to even Bahasa Indonesia, one can communicate rather basically and see success. Therefore, I learned that if a meal or experience was good, I could say **bagus**. If it was really good, I could simply repeat it and say **bagus, bagus**. To say that something is beautiful you can say **indah** and if it's really gorgeous you can say **indah, indah**. There are other words that could be used to communicate the superlatives of good and beautiful, but doubling the word is most effective when one wants to communicate with guaranteed success. When we come to Isaiah 6, I am reminded of those language studies on Borneo.

Above him were seraphim, each with six wings:
With two wings they covered their faces,
with two they covered their feet,
and with two they were flying.
And they were calling to one another:
"Holy, holy, holy is the Lord Almighty;
the whole earth is full of his glory."

Isaiah 6:2-3

The significance of this repetition of the word "holy" is unmissable. God is so transcendent in his holiness that the word "holy" does not suffice in our description of him. He is holy. And holy. And holy. But that repetition is still insufficient so the angels go on to call out that the WHOLE earth is FULL of his glory. That's holy! And then notice that the angels have wings for more than flying: two wings covered their faces and two covered their feet. What a picture of the holiness of our God and our own unworthiness to be in his presence. Even the angels had to protect themselves from looking upon God and from standing on holy ground. That's holy.

There are two more details to notice, here.

Firstly, the angels are not singing TO the Lord – seated, high and exalted, on the throne. They are calling out the truth of who he is TO ONE ANOTHER. As mentioned in the introduction to this book, we truly cannot fully worship in isolation. We need to call out our praises of our Almighty Lord to each other. It's mathematical, really – a multiplication of praise!

Secondly, notice Isaiah's response to what he saw.

"Woe to me!" I cried. "I am ruined! For I am a man of unclean lips,
and I live among a people of unclean lips,
and my eyes have seen the King, the Lord Almighty."
Isaiah 6:5

I get it. I think I understand his response. When we truly see the holiness of Almighty God, we are "undone" as it says in the King James Version. We are ruined. The transcendence of God is so extreme that we are forced to our knees before Holy God.

We see an image similar to Isaiah's in John's book of Revelation. Again, there is the triple repetition to signify the infinite holiness of God. As the oft-used expression in sci-fi books and movies goes – to infinity and beyond!

And the four living creatures, each of them with six wings,
are full of eyes all around and within, and day and night
they never cease to say, "Holy, holy, holy, is the Lord God Almighty,
who was and is and is to come!"

Revelation 4:8 ESV

Holy, holy, holy!
Lord God Almighty
Early in the morning
Our song shall rise to Thee
Holy, holy, holy!
Merciful and mighty
God in three persons
Blessed Trinity!
Holy, holy, holy!
Though the darkness hide thee
Though the eye of sinful man
Thy glory may not see
Only Thou art holy
There is none beside Thee
Perfect in power, in love and purity

Reginald Heber[56]

Perfection

My memory bank is packed to the brim with memories of perfect moments. The beauty of our memory is that the actual flaws that were in those moments tend to fade over time. As our memories fail us, we tend to only remember the extremes. It is, evidently, related to the various hormones that are activated in our bodies in an extremely fabulous or extremely fearsome moment. Without the mundane pieces of the moment, the extremely great moments become more extremely great over time. Funny how that works.

When we began our look into God's holiness, I asked you to think of the most perfect person you knew. Maybe the idea of perfection is where we need to land in our understanding of holiness. Though many of us bear that label of "perfectionist", we, regrettably, are not perfect. We might strive for it. We might dream of it. But just ask a perfectionist how perfect their last project ended up being… you'll see. Perfectionists can point out every flaw in their work. How can they enjoy the results when they want perfection but can't achieve it? Ahhhhh, therein lies the struggle.

Many perfectionists have learned to adapt. My daughter-in-law, Meyling, is a great example. She has embraced minimalism in her home and life. She spends very little time putting away stuff because she got rid of that stuff, altogether. But she would say that there is always a tension between wanting perfect simplicity and finding it. I have observed her handle that tension very well. Yet it remains a very real tension.

1999 was the year that I determined, because of that tension, to embrace the phrase - "Oh well, bummer". I journaled about my commitment to use the phrase and I practiced saying it and writing it... over and over. I always had such high expectations for myself and others that I never seemed satisfied. I was always striving. You ask how that's worked for me? I've not been perfect in my use of that phrase, but – oh well, bummer!

This tension is true for many... not for God. He doesn't ever strive for anything. Striving involves an expense of energy and God doesn't lose energy. We'll get to that more in a later chapter. My point, here, is that God is the only successful perfectionist. Once we realise that, we can let ourselves off the hook. Release the pressure. Our results aren't perfect, but we can still appreciate those results. And God's results are always perfect. Therefore, all of our worship is, deservedly, meant to be toward him.

The full picture

It's time to pull together all of the aspects of God's holiness and look at the full picture. Holiness involves wholeness, complete health with no presence of flaws. It involves purity, a morality that is so pure that there is absolutely no presence of any sin or of anything short of perfection. God is pure, not just in his actions but also in his intentions, his motives. Holiness involves being "other" – distinct and set apart from all that is unholy. And the holiness of God involves a transcendence that is vastly beyond any qualities found in humanity. God's transcendence is a majesty, a glory that places him far above all false gods, all spiritual powers, all humans, and all of creation. God is absolutely and morally pure while he is absolutely and majestically awesome.

Be holy. Me?

> *"I am the Lord your God; consecrate yourselves*
> *and be holy, because I am holy.*
> *Do not make yourselves unclean by any creature that moves along the ground.*
> *I am the Lord, who brought you up out of Egypt to be your God;*
> *therefore be holy, because I am holy."*
>
> **Leviticus 11:44-45**

> *As obedient children, do not conform to the evil desires*
> *you had when you lived in ignorance.*
> *But just as he who called you is holy,*
> *so be holy in all you do;*
> *for it is written: "Be holy, because I am holy."*
>
> **1 Peter 1:14-16**

Really, God? You expect me to be holy? In both the Old and New Testaments, we read exactly that. God requires us to be holy. The more I grasp tiny pieces of an understanding of God's holiness, the more I am in total agreement with the prophet's words we read earlier in Isaiah 6. I am undone. But isn't it curious that the more we are aware of our unholiness, the more we seek God's face rather than turn away from his face? And of course, that's the way he meant it to be. When we realise that we are not able to be holy, we turn to The One who is fully able.

If we think we can be holy on our own, we'll try. Just check out the history of the Church for some stories of tragic attempts at holiness –

sitting on a pillar high above everyone's heads in the midst of a desert, not for days but for years; self-flagellation, whipping one's own body (often one's back) to the point that bloody stripes appear on the skin; the dangerous deprivation of food and water that went far beyond basic fasting. Please don't misunderstand me; I am not against all monastic traditions. There is a part of me that is always drawn to the serenity, simplicity and single-mindedness of life in a monastery. I actually love visiting ancient monasteries and often listen to Gregorian chant. (Just ask my students when I taught Church History; they were introduced to such music whether they wanted to be or not!) Many times, over the years, I've practised silence and solitude. Usually, only a day at a time, however. And a friend and I are hoping to soon book a weekend at a retreat centre that is open for such purposes.

However, remember in the chapter on God's grace when we looked at spiritual disciplines a bit. I gave the following definition for these disciplines – something we can do by direct effort that enables us to do what we can't do by direct effort. Doing things that a monk might choose to do is not, in itself, being holy. But following some of those disciplines puts us in a place of surrender and dependence on the Only One who can make us holy. When the Holy Spirit is the one at work, amazing things can happen. Our hearts and minds can be transformed – that's the "be holy" part of the verse. And out of that transformation comes obedience to God's Word and the "holy in all you do" that follows. Look back to Peter's opening thoughts at the beginning of his letter.

> *...To God's elect, exiles scattered throughout the provinces of Pontus, Galatia, Cappadocia, Asia and Bithynia, who have been chosen according to the foreknowledge of God the Father, **through the sanctifying work of the Spirit**, to be obedient to Jesus Christ and sprinkled with his blood: grace and peace be yours in abundance.*
>
> **1 Peter 1:1-2, emphasis added**

Before Peter reminds us that we are to be holy in our behaviour, he reminds us of our source. The word which is translated "sanctifying" in this verse is from the root word for "holy". Since "sanctify" isn't a regular part of our vocabulary, this could more easily read, "through the Spirit's work in making us holy." Once again, I am relieved to know that it is the Holy Spirit who does the work of making me more and more holy as I am more and more willing to surrender.

> *If we're heading for a holy city, clearly holiness is our end. If holiness is our ultimate aim and our foreordained goal, then holiness must be the dominant theme of our lives on our journey.*
>
> **Stuart and Jill Briscoe**[57]

[57] Stuart and Jill Briscoe, *Life, Liberty, and the Pursuit of Holiness*, Scripture Press, 1993, p. 160.

If I wonder why something trying is allowed, and press for prayer that it may be removed; if I cannot be trusted with any disappointment, and cannot go on in peace under any mystery, then I know nothing of Calvary love.

Amy Carmichael[58]

If you will withdraw yourself from worthless conversations and from roaming about idly, as well as from listening to new things and rumors, you will find enough free time that is suitable for meditation on good things.

Thomas à Kempis[59]

For Reflection

1. Look online for a recorded version of the hymn that is found a few pages earlier: **Holy, Holy, Holy**. It bears repeating. Meditate on the lyrics as you listen to the strong cadence, the melody and the harmonies.

2. What is it about considering the holiness of God that causes you to want to hide from him? He knows and he understands. So, bring those concerns to him in prayer.

3. Is it time for you to embrace a spiritual discipline? A day of solitude, perhaps? Determine a date, time and place for some solitude. Bring your Bible, a journal and pen, some water… and soak in the bubble bath of God's goodness.

4. *Earth's crammed with heaven, And every common bush afire with God, But only he who sees take off his shoes; The rest sit 'round and pick blackberries.*
   Elizabeth Barrett Browning[60]

Above wide glass doors that open onto our Hinterland-facing deck, a friend painted the words, which are written above, from one of my favourite poems. For one week, make an intentional decision to notice all of the "common bushes" that are afire with God. It is holy ground. No matter where you are when you see that "bush" – "take off your shoes", enter into the holy moment and turn your face toward God. Pause. Write about it. Or speak to a friend about it. Or, even better, invite someone to do this week-long exercise with you!

9

GOD IS RIGHTEOUS

*At last meditating day and night,
by the mercy of God,
I... began to understand that the righteousness
of God is that through
which the righteous live by a gift of God,
namely by faith...
Here I felt as if I were entirely born again and
had entered paradise itself through the gates
that had been flung open.*

Martin Luther

Martin Luther, one of the great Protestant reformers of the 1500s, struggled with the "both/and" of mercy and righteousness. (Both/and means that mercy and righteousness are not "either/or" choices.) As a devout monk, he forced intense suffering upon his body, depriving himself of food, water and protection for extended periods of time. In brutal German winters he was known for sleeping outside, wearing limited clothing and lying on the frozen and barren ground. He beat himself – physically, emotionally and spiritually. He is known to have said, "If anyone could have earned heaven by the life of a monk, it was I." The young Martin Luther was tormented by Romans 1:17, "For in the gospel the righteousness of God is revealed—a righteousness that is by faith from first to last, just as it is written: 'The righteous will live by faith.'" He desperately wanted to live by faith, but he was well aware of his own lack of righteousness. For Luther, everything changed while he was studying the book of Romans and finally understood the full meaning of chapter 1. The faith by which the righteous live is not faith in our own righteousness but, rather, faith in the very righteousness of God.

This gloomy idea that the only solution for self-love is self-hatred and self-accusation was built upon a frightening view of God. Luther could only see that God was all Judge and no love, his righteousness being all about punishing sinners, his 'gospel' just the promise of judgment. Here was a God he could only ever cower before. Then, in 1519, when he was looking again at the issues of confession and repentance, it struck him that, after the sinner had confessed, the priest would pronounce God's promise of forgiveness. It was a whole new way of looking at things for Luther; now, the question was, would the sinner trust God's promise? And with that, everything changed. Now he saw that forgiveness is not dependent on how certain the sinner is that he has been truly contrite; forgiveness comes simply by receiving the promise of God. Thus the sinner's hope is found, not in himself, but outside himself, in God's word of promise.

Michael Reeves[61]

---

[61] Michael Reeves, *The Unquenchable Flame, Discovering the Heart of the Reformation*, The Society of Promoting Christian Knowledge, Inter-Varsity Press, U.K., 2009, pp. 46-47. Reproduced with permission of the Licensor through PLSclear.

Grasping the reality of God's righteousness should not lead us to a fear of failure but to immense relief and gratitude. Relief – that it is not our righteousness that saves us for we would all, surely, fail. Gratitude – that the righteous forgiveness of our Lord Jesus Christ is what saves us.

Further Explanation

So, what does it mean to be righteous? There's no quick answer to that. Honestly, I debated about including "righteousness" in the next chapter on "justice". Though righteousness and justice often appear together, especially in the Old Testament, I believe each word needs to be handled on its own. And I believe that there is an aspect of this word "righteous" that places it right between holiness and justice with overlap on both sides.

Righteousness is about a standard, a perfect standard that often leads to righteous, or just, deeds. The word cluster for this word in Hebrew includes various forms of **tzedaqah.** It refers to a standard of rightness. But in addition to a right standard, it is a word that involves right relationships. The Bible Project has some excellent discussion around the differences between "just" and "righteous". (If you've not checked them out by this chapter, please drop everything and do so![62]) **Tzedaqah** is similar to the phrase we have in English - do right by me/you/him/her. It is the standard between two people, or between two parties of any size, that causes one side or both sides to do right by the other party.

> *Righteousness is a core component of the gospel message.*
> *The holy and eternal God expects that [sic] people who are in relationship*
> *with him to be without sin. This is, as we all know,*
> *a requirement that is utterly impossible for any of us*
> *to meet on our own. However, in the gospel, God*
> *delivers his righteousness to unrighteous people*
> *without sacrificing his own righteousness in the process.*
>
> **The Jesus Bible**[63]

The book of Romans

The New Testament letter from Paul to the Church in Rome is packed with explanations on righteousness and justice. In the opening chapters of Romans, Paul makes it clear that God always does what is right and he is faithful to fulfil his promises. This idea of being faithful to his promises links us back to our discussion on **hesed** and our covenant-keeping God. It also brings up many of the ideas we handled when looking into God's faithfulness. Our covenant-keeping God is faithfully loyal to his people and to his promises.

The truth Luther encountered in chapter 1 of Romans is developed further in chapter 3 when, in verse 10, we read that there is no one who is righteous. Not even one. Clearly, it is quite silly to ever consider depending upon our own righteousness. Our only hope is in Jesus.

---

[63] *The Jesus Bible*, NIV, editor in chief: Louie Giglio, Zondervan, 2016, notes, p. 1751. Used by permission.

> *Therefore, since we have been justified through faith,*
> *we have peace with God through our Lord Jesus Christ,*
> *through whom we have gained access by faith into this grace*
> *in which we now stand. And we boast in the hope of the glory of God.*
> **Romans 5:1-2**

Let's look more closely, for a moment, at what Paul is clarifying that brought so much freedom to Martin Luther so long ago. Because we are declared to be righteous, because we are "justified", we are accepted into relationship with God through the righteousness of Jesus Christ.

That word "justified" becomes quite confusing in the present day because of the way we tend to use it to refer to having an excuse. One might say that they were "justified" in their anger because someone broke something that was precious to them. So, "I am justified" means "I have a good excuse". Due to lack of time to travel down a bunny trail, let's just say that having a reason for an emotion is not the same as having an excuse for an action. We might have a valid reason to be upset and yet not have any excuse for our harmful thinking and actions that follow. Attempts at justifying our sin fail to remove its sinfulness. Does that make sense? Justification uses terms like "you made me" when, in actuality, no one can force us to feel a certain way and act upon that feeling.

Now back to this Biblical term – justification. To be justified means to be called righteous. It's unlike the over-simplified expression you may have been taught (and that I might have used more than once, myself) –

"Justification means just as if you never sinned." Oh no! Apologies for those statements from decades ago! Justification is far more than the absence of sin. The sin truly existed, the price had to be paid, and the price has been paid by Jesus' death on the cross. Justification is so much more than the absence of sin because it means that the perfection of the Son of God, the Lamb of God who takes away the sin of the world, has been put on your financial account so that the price is fully paid. You and I are declared, not "just" absent of sin, but full of righteousness. I love the easy-language way this is described by Eugene Peterson in **The Message.**

Christ arrives right on time to make this happen. He didn't, and doesn't, wait for us to get ready. He presented himself for this sacrificial death when we were far too weak and rebellious to do anything to get ourselves ready.
And even if we hadn't been so weak, we wouldn't have known what to do anyway. We can understand someone dying for a person worth dying for, and we can understand how someone good and noble could inspire us to selfless sacrifice. But God put his love on the line for us by offering his Son in sacrificial death while we were of no use whatever to him.
Romans 5:6-8 MSG

Jesus became what he was not – so that we could become what we were not. Jesus became sin so that we could become righteous. The result is that wrongs are made right. We have a right relationship with God, are a rightful part of the family of God, and we have a right future because of the opportunity to be transformed by the grace of God. As followers of Jesus, our righteousness is a gift, a declaration of who we are because of the cross of Christ.

Peter's example

I am forever comforted by the accounts of Peter with Jesus. The patience of Jesus toward the impulsive Peter is particularly reassuring to someone of my temperament who has, at times, been known to speak before thinking. God's goodness and mercy and grace and compassion and patience and love and faithfulness are all fully operational alongside his holiness and his righteousness. There is no heartless standard of right-ness in God. That would not fit into his character. Jesus didn't say anything close to this: "Peter, you'll be declared righteous if you don't sink in the water due to lack of faith, if you don't lop off a guy's ear in anger, if you don't deny me three times out of fear."[64]

Because of all that God is, we find a very different Peter when he wrote his two letters, 1 and 2 Peter.

Therefore, with minds that are alert and fully sober, set your hope on the grace to be brought to you when Jesus Christ is revealed at his coming. As obedient children, do not conform to the evil desires you had when you lived in ignorance. But just as he who called you is holy, so be holy in all you do; for it is written: "Be holy, because I am holy."
1 Peter 1:13-16

---

[64] References for each occurrence in order mentioned: Matthew 14:22-33, John 18:10, Luke 22:54-62.

A bit about clothing

We'll deal with the link between righteousness and justice in the next chapter. I'll wrap up this little chapter with one more thought about righteousness. Righteousness is what we wear. As followers of Jesus, righteousness is our new identity. It is our very being, not because of anything innate in our original and sinful state but because of grace.

I delight greatly in the Lord, my soul rejoices in my God.
For he has clothed me with garments of salvation and arrayed me in a robe
of his righteousness, as a bridegroom adorns his head like a priest,
and as a bride adorns herself with her jewels.

Isaiah 61:10

That's what enabled Peter to be so transformed. It was not his own righteousness that we see exhibited in the powerful writing in his letters. He was wearing a robe of righteousness. That's grace. Amazing.

For Reflection

1. Read Romans 10:1-10 and Philippians 3:2-9. Using any kind of notation device, which could include creating a chart that compares the two passages, note the contrasting elements of God's righteousness and our own righteousness.

2. If you've been a Christian for quite a long time, you might have (as I sometimes have) begun to think that God got a pretty good deal when he got you! Justification is not just as if you never sinned. You were a complete sinner and yet God's righteousness met his mercy at the cross of Christ. Thank God for his rescuing work in your life.

3. 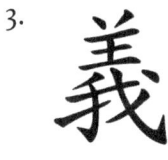 The ancient Mandarin Chinese depiction of the concept of "righteousness" is fascinating. It is written like a fraction with the word for "lamb" over the word for "me". Consider that. Journal about that. Or, if research is more your style, do some studying of this ancient word. Impactful, right?!

4. Read Peter's message to the crowd in Acts 2:14-41. The fearful disciple who couldn't admit that he knew Jesus, even to a servant girl by a fire in the High Priest's courtyard, is this man who boldly proclaimed Jesus to a huge gathering of sceptics! Consider that the same transformation is available in your life. Talk with God about the longings of your heart to surrender fully to his transformation.

10
GOD IS JUST

Righteousness and justice are the foundation of your throne; love and faithfulness go before you.

Psalm 89:14

This is what the Lord says: "Let not the wise boast of their wisdom or the strong boast of their strength or the rich boast of their riches, but let the one who boasts boast about this: that they have the understanding to know me, that I am the Lord, who exercises kindness, justice and righteousness on earth, for in these delight," declares the Lord.

Jeremiah 9:23-24

"But let justice roll on like a river, righteousness like a never-failing stream."

Amos 5:24

The above verses demonstrate what I mentioned in the previous chapter about how commonly these words are together – justice and righteousness. **Mishpat,** the Hebrew word that is usually translated "justice", occurs, in its many forms, more than 200 times in the Old Testament. **Tzedaqah,** the Hebrew word "justice" that is most often translated "righteousness" and which we talked about more extensively in the previous chapter, refers to a right standard and right relationships. These two words are used in combination with each other in the Old Testament close to 40 times. When used together, there is one English term that best encapsulates both concepts – social justice.

The crux of justice

Before we dig into the blend of **mishpat** and **tzedaqah**, of social justice, let's remind ourselves of the foundational truth of God's justice as profoundly evidenced in the crucifixion!

> *...the crucifixion is the apex of God's love and mercy but also of his justice and righteousness. At the cross, God not only provided the ultimate answer for how a person can be made righteous by faith, but he also dispensed his justice. ...*
> *At the cross, the God of righteousness both demonstrates and grants righteousness, for he is both just and the One who justifies.*
> **The Jesus Bible**[65]

At the cross of Christ, mercy and justice walk hand in hand. And that has been the way of God since before the beginning of humanity's time.

> *We should banish from our minds forever the common but erroneous notion that justice and judgment characterize the God of Israel, while mercy and grace belong to the Lord of the Church. Actually there is in principle no difference between the Old Testament and the New. In the New Testament Scriptures there is a fuller development*

---

[65] *The Jesus Bible*, NIV, editor in chief: Louie Giglio, Zondervan, 2016, notes, p.1751. Used by permission.

> *of redemptive truth, but one God speaks in both…*
> *Whether in the Garden of Eden or the Garden of Gethsemane,*
> *God is merciful as well as just. He has always dealt in mercy with mankind*
> *and will always deal in justice when His mercy is despised.*
>
> **A.W. Tozer**[66]

I am so incredibly grateful that it is God's nature to care for the helpless. Because of my sin as a part of humanity, I was born helpless. That was my nature. God's nature causes him to help; our nature causes us to need his help. No amount of godly parenting by my family could make me anything but helpless when it comes to the things that matter most. I learned how to walk and how to talk, how to feed myself, how to behave around my elders (a phrase limited to certain eras and cultures)… because my parents taught me. But, even then, I needed Jesus in order to deal with my sinfulness. I am grateful for the cross. In it, I have found life – both everlasting life and abundant life. My future is secure and my present can be full of purpose and victory. Here are a few of the many profound lyrics from a song by Hillsong Music that reminds us that while we're waiting, we're not waiting.

> *Whether now or then*
> *Death is not my end*
> **_I know Heaven waits for me_**
> *I know You love me*
> *I know You found me*
> *I know You saved me*
> *And Your grace will never fail me*
> *And while I'm waiting*

---

[66] A.W. Tozer, *The Knowledge of the Holy*, Harper & Row, 1961, 1975 edition, p. 97.

> *I'm not waiting*
> *<u>I</u> <u>know</u> <u>Heaven</u> <u>lives</u> <u>in</u> <u>me</u>*[67]
> **(emphasis added)**

Just is fair

When he was young, one of our two sons (I'll leave him unnamed; you'll have a 50/50 chance of making the wrong guess so don't bother guessing!) quite often used a particular phrase when it came to discipline – "That's not fair!" Even now, I can almost hear the whiny frustration in his voice. After the initial declaration, he would go on to explain that, in his opinion, I was much too tough on him and had just been much too lenient with his brother. And I would, sometimes patiently and sometimes not so, explain that in order to be fair I needed to do what each child needed so that their discipline was effective in helping them to become the person God wanted them to be. And that meant disciplining them differently, according to what would make the greatest impact on each precious personality and temperament. Just is fair. Equal value; differing responses. It might not be the same action or response with each person and it might not even be the same action or response in each situation with the same person, but just is fair.

For the record, this dear son of mine did grow out of that stage and I'm pleased to report that he uses much of the same concept with his own children, in his own way. He knows each child so well that he knows what each one, individually, needs in order to grow.

---

[67] *As It Is (In Heaven)*, Words and Music by Joel Houston & Ben Fielding, © 2016 Hillsong Music Publishing. Used by permission.

This is an imperfect picture of the perfectly just and merciful choices God makes in response to the sin of each human and of each people group. He might seem so patient with one group of people and so impatient with another. In reality, God is incredibly patient with each of us throughout history. It's okay to check back on the details in the chapter on God's patience, if you need to remind yourself. I need to remind myself. Often. And please understand that I am not addressing, at this point, the whole question of evil and suffering in the world. We will deal with that a bit in the chapter on God's sovereignty.

In the book of Lamentations, written by the prophet Jeremiah, we see this tension of justice/fairness/equality played out. To lament is to honestly express grief and sorrow. The book of Psalms contains many songs of lament. When I have been struggling in a particularly tough situation, some of those psalms have become my friends. They give voice to the feelings that I can't seem to express on my own. Almost the entire book of Lamentations is a lament. And yet... right in the middle of it we find the well-known passage, which we considered in the chapter on God's faithfulness. Here it is in another version.

God's loyal love couldn't have run out, his merciful love
couldn't have dried up. They're created new every morning.
How great your faithfulness!
I'm sticking with God (I say it over and over). He's all I've got left.
Lamentations 3:22-24 MSG

We see the same pattern, here, in the psalms of lament as well. Even in the midst of our emoting we still know, and need to remind ourselves of, the truth of who God is. He is good, even in the midst.

---

*Lamentations may seem like a book that is full of strong
sorrow and bitterness, and through most of the book, it is.
The prophet Jeremiah continually complained about the plight of the city,
and he was distraught at how the Lord had brought judgment upon his people.
However, it is important to note that these complaints are never against God.
Jeremiah was certainly upset about the situation,
but there was no suggestion that God's judgment was somehow unjust.*
The Jesus Bible[68]

---

*But it happened because of the sins of her prophets
and the iniquities of her priests, who shed within
her the blood of the righteous.*
Lamentations 4:13

Jeremiah never questioned why God was allowing destruction on the city of Jerusalem. He knew that the people and their leaders had rebelled against God. Justice was being served. Even at the end of the lament, Jeremiah asks God to bring the restoration of their relationship with him. Justice is fair. And fair justice can bring restoration.

Back to that parenting illustration for a moment. Those of you who are parents would agree, I'm sure, that there is no greater joy in the tough

---

[68] The Jesus Bible, NIV, editor in chief: Louie Giglio, Zondervan, 2016, notes, p.1268. Used by permission.

moments of parenting than to experience restoration of a full and fun-filled relationship with our children... after their repentance. When our children were old enough to reason through rather difficult concepts, I stopped telling them that they must apologise to whomever they had wronged. I'm sure that we all have a memory of some child (in my case, it's me!) who was forced to apologise and, therefore, with head bent toward the floor and with a snarl on their face, they said to the harmed party, "Sorry", in a tone of only mild disgust. Mild lest they be forced, by a parent, to say it again a bit kindlier.

That is why I always told the child in need that I was praying that they would feel godly sorrow that would lead them to repentance and to the appropriate apologies (2 Corinthians 7:10). And I often would check in with them to see if they were genuinely ready to apologise. But I didn't want to raise hypocrites who looked good on the outside yet were hardened on the inside. When they used the word "sorry", I prayed that it would come out of true sorrow. Then it would mean that even though they were initially only sorry that they got caught, finally they were sorry for what they had done.

Better, yet, were the times when my child was grateful that they were caught and they easily repented. And an even greater joy was felt by all when that child confessed what they'd done before they were discovered. Sometimes there still needed to be discipline but it was in a much more joyous context of restoration. In those instances when I had to pray a long time before that godly sorrow exhibited itself, what a joy it was when it finally did.

So, in the context of the sins of his nation, how delightful it is that Jeremiah asked God to bring restoration. His lament included his sorrow over the sin of his people. And how just of God to respond with love. Just is fair. Again. Still.

The uniqueness of our God

In most ancient civilisations, the gods were associated with the powerful. Kings and rulers were channels of power from the gods to the privileged. The underprivileged were expected to submit to that power. They were not expected to benefit from it. But throughout the Old Testament, we see that the God who rescued the slaves out of Egypt was deeply committed to the welfare of the underprivileged.

For a thorough unpacking of God's justice and our response to it, I recommend Timothy Keller's book, **Generous Justice**[69] – and I should warn you – prepare to be stretched!

...the Bible says that God is the defender of the poor; it never says he is the defender of the rich. And while some texts call for justice for members of the well-off classes as well, the calls to render justice to the poor outnumber such passages by a hundred to one. Why? Rich people can certainly be treated unjustly, but philosopher Nicholas Wolterstorff says it is a simple fact that the lower classes are "not only disproportionately vulnerable to injustice, but usually disproportionately actual victims of injustice. Injustice is not equally distributed." It stands to reason that the injustice is easier to perform against people without the money or social status to defend themselves.
Timothy Keller[70]

The quartet of the vulnerable

Nicholas Wolterstorff, quoted by Timothy Keller, above, coined a term

---

[69] Timothy Keller, *Generous Justice: How God's Grace Makes Us Just*, first published: Dutton, 2010, Hodder & Stoughton Ltd, 2018 edition.
[70] Ibid, p. 7.

for those we might call underprivileged – "the quartet of the vulnerable" – widows, orphans, immigrants and the poor. As evidenced by the many times this grouping appears together in the Bible, this quartet is clearly a focus of concern for our God. Scripture makes it quite obvious that it is to be our concern as well.

For the Lord your God is God of gods and Lord of lords, the great God, mighty and awesome, who shows no partiality and accepts no bribes. He defends the cause of the fatherless and the widow, and loves the foreigner residing among you, giving them food and clothing.

Deuteronomy 10:17-18

He upholds the cause of the oppressed and gives food to the hungry. The Lord sets prisoners free, the Lord gives sight to the blind, the Lord lifts up those who are bowed down, the Lord loves the righteous. The Lord watches over the foreigner and sustains the fatherless and the widow, but he frustrates the ways of the wicked.

Psalm 146:7-9

Woe to those who make unjust laws, to those who issue oppressive decrees, to deprive the poor of their rights and withhold justice from the oppressed of my people, making widows their prey and robbing the fatherless.

Isaiah 10:1-2

This is what the Lord Almighty said: "Administer true justice; show mercy and compassion to one another. Do not oppress the widow or the fatherless, the foreigner or the poor. Do not plot evil against each other."

Zechariah 7:9-10

The New Testament Church

You might be surprised to find far fewer occurrences of "justice" in our English New Testaments than in the Old Testament. Most of those occurrences are a form of the Greek root word, **krino,** which leans more toward judgement and evaluation. However, if you include a search for the word translated "righteous" you'll see "justice" all over the New Testament. This is the Greek word cluster, **dikaiosune.** Though it is translated "righteous" it carries a deeper meaning similar to "well-ordering" that includes a broad view of justice. In fact, our English word "righteous" was originally spelled "rihtwis" in Old English. Therefore, both the Greek and the Old English get us back to the Hebrew word, **tzedaqah**, we discussed in the previous chapter. "Righteous" is a standard, a straight or right way, to be toward and to act toward another human.

One of the ways the early Church "turned the world upside down" (Acts 17:6 NKJV) was by offering justice to the marginalised. Though their fasting was, firstly, for spiritual reasons, when they fasted, they were able to have more money or food available to help the underprivileged. What they didn't eat that day could help someone else. That kind of giving was viewed as their privilege. Sometimes, as we see below, those who were property owners sold their property in order to help someone in need.

All the believers were one in heart and mind. No one claimed that any of their possessions was their own, but they shared everything they had. With great power the apostles continued to testify to the resurrection of

> *the Lord Jesus. And God's grace was so powerfully at work in them all*
> *that there were no needy persons among them.*
> *For from time to time those who owned land or houses sold them,*
> *brought the money from the sales and put it at the apostles' feet,*
> *and it was distributed to anyone who had need.*
> **Acts 4:32-35**

Jesus, himself, established this priority of caring for the marginalised and underprivileged. In the well-known parable that is often called The Good Samaritan, Jesus makes his point quite clear.

> *"Which of these three do you think was a neighbor to the man*
> *who fell into the hands of robbers?" The expert in the law replied,*
> *"The one who had mercy on him." Jesus told him, "Go and do likewise."*
> **Luke 10:36-37**

And then, not long before the crucifixion, Jesus again clarifies the importance of caring for the marginalised.

> *"'For I was hungry and you gave me something to eat,*
> *I was thirsty and you gave me something to drink,*
> *I was a stranger and you invited me in, I needed clothes and you clothed me,*
> *I was sick and you looked after me, I was in prison and you came to visit me.'*
> *Then the righteous will answer him, 'Lord, when did we see you hungry and*
> *feed you, or thirsty and give you something to drink? When did we see you a*
> *stranger and invite you in, or needing clothes and clothe you?*
> *When did we see you sick or in prison and go to visit you?'*

> *The King will reply, 'Truly I tell you, whatever you did for one of the least of these brothers and sisters of mine, you did for me.'"*
> **Matthew 25:35-40**

The many faces of justice

Many Biblical thinkers have developed an idea of two types of justice, which are common today and relate to the two Hebrew words we've discussed. These terms are "primary justice" and "rectifying justice". I appreciate the point made, below, that rectifying justice would not even be necessary in the world if primary justice was the norm.

> *Rectifying justice is **mishpat**. It means punishing wrong-doers and caring for the victims of unjust treatment.*
> *Primary justice, or **tzedaqah**, is behavior that, if it was prevalent in the world, would render rectifying justice unnecessary,*
> *because everyone would be living in right relationship to everyone else.*
> **Timothy Keller**[71]

Social justice today

This is not the place to flesh out the "how" of social justice. Is the manna that was provided to all Israelites equally, no matter the capacity of some to gather more than others, an image of successful socialism? Do the gleaning laws of the Old Testament support the idea that the poor will always be with us, and therefore support capitalism? If so,

---
[71] Ibid, p. 16.

what about the notion of not harvesting every speck of grain but, rather, leaving a generous amount for the poor? Is serving the poor a function of the Church, the State, both? Timothy Keller has devoted an entire book, many articles, many podcasts and many videos to this topic. In his book, he addresses the causes of poverty and what it means to "do justice" so I refer you to any one of those valuable resources for further study. (See the following page for more options.)

I simply want to make it clear that, from God's perspective, justice is for all. And justice for the vulnerable, for those least apt to typically receive justice, is of primary importance to our God who is a just God. The total times that the two Hebrew words for justice and the two Greek words for justice are used in Scripture is over 1500 times! That's twice as many times as words for heaven occur and seven times as often as we find words for hell. Justice is central in the heart of God.

This requires that we make extra effort to determine where injustice exists, that we work hard to punish wrong-doers, that we make every effort to assist victims of injustice, and that we all seek to live in right relationships whenever it is in our power to do so. Because God is just.

He has shown you, O mortal, what is good.
And what does the Lord require of you? To act justly
and to love mercy and to walk humbly with your God.

Micah 6:8

For Reflection

1. Listen to one of the full versions of Hillsong's *As It Is (In Heaven)*. My personal favourite is an acoustic version. They can be found on YouTube. Consider the lyrics in the context of God's justice and mercy toward you.

2. Meditate on Jeremiah 9:23-24. Think through the characteristics of God that are described in these verses. Write a response.

3. Are you "in the midst"? Are you in the middle of a situation for which you see no end in sight? Write your own lament. If you need help getting started, read Psalm 42 and use it as a framework for your own words. Notice verses 5 and 11. In your lament, are you able to include a phrase about still desiring to put your hope in God? If not, talk with God about that need. He can handle your honesty. Reach out to a friend who can support you in your season of lament. Pray with them.

4. If time does not allow you to read Timothy Keller's book, **Generous Justice**, listen to one of his sermons on God's justice on your favourite podcast app or on YouTube. Also, there are many excellent books that specifically deal with racial injustice. Whatever our shade of skin, we have much to learn. Personally, I've had to recognise the privilege that has been mine for my entire life. Might I suggest a few great titles, wherever you are on the justice journey? You may not agree with everything that is said, but I believe it will widen your eyes and your heart.

- Bryan Stevenson, **Just Mercy: A Story of Justice and Redemption**, Spiegel and Grau, 2014.
- Jemar Tisby, **The Color of Compromise: The Truth about the American Church's Complicity in Racism,** Zondervan, 2019.
- Benjamin Watson, **Under Our Skin: Getting Real about Race. Getting Free from the Fears and Frustrations that Divide Us.** Tyndale Momentum, 2015.

PART THREE

His Greatness

11

GOD IS ALL-POWERFUL

*Since He has at His command all the power in the universe,
the Lord God omnipotent can do anything as easily as anything else.
All His acts are done without effort. He expends no energy that
must be replenished. His self-sufficiency makes it unnecessary for
Him to look outside of Himself for a renewal of strength.
All the power required to do all that He wills to do
lies in undiminished fullness in His own infinite being.*

A.W. Tozer[72]

We have now fully shifted into considering the attributes of God that belong to God, alone. We begin with God's omnipotence, his all-powerfulness. Though we are able to grow in our likeness to Jesus, the characteristics of God, which we will explore in the next few chapters are not characteristics that we will begin to take on, ourselves. When I look into any attribute of God, my response must always be, "You are God. I am not." That reality is never in question. In case we think otherwise, these attributes remind us of that truth!

When you and I face something BIG that requires strength, we speak in these terms: sweat, muscles, grunts, groans, exertion, exhaustion, oomph. Consider this – none of those words can be used to describe our God. Absolutely none. If that's not overwhelming, here are some more words that cannot ever apply to God's strength: inhale, recover, restore, rest, refill, refuel, rebuild…. I don't know about you but I need to sit a bit, inhale and exhale, and recover from just writing that list. This truth of God overwhelms me. And that's another word that does not, and cannot, apply to God – "overwhelmed"! God is never overwhelmed. Ever.

We, as created beings, are so limited in our grasp of the things beyond us. Our Creator is definitely far beyond us. But it's still worth the effort to try to grasp some more realities about God's power.

The Creator

Energy is a function of our universe. The Laws of Thermodynamics are a part of creation; they are not inherent in our Creator. Strength is a function of our universe. Force, pressure and muscle mass are a part of creation; they are not a part of the Creator. The very fact that this is mind-boggling to me and to you reminds us that we are definitely not like God! Our brains lack the power to even grasp the reality of the immense power of God.

By the word of the Lord the heavens were made,
their starry host by the breath of his mouth.
He gathers the waters of the sea into jars;
he puts the deep into storehouses.
Let all the earth fear the Lord;

> *let all the people of the world revere him.*
> *For he spoke, and it came to be;*
> *he commanded, and it stood firm.*
>
> **Psalm 33:6-9**

The above psalm echoes the pictures in the creation account found in the book of Genesis, chapter 1. To exemplify the strength of Almighty God, the writers use a picture of God speaking the world into existence. In reality, words aren't even necessary in order for God to create. His power requires nothing, not even words.

But humanity, created in the image of the Creator yet still quite unlike him, requires words in order to try to grasp God's power in creation. As I write, the words of a "powerful" (used in a Spirit-anointed way and not a human way) anthem is the soundtrack of my mind. Here's just a sampling of the lyrics.

> *God of creation*
> *There at the start*
> *Before the beginning of time*
> *With no point of reference*
> *You spoke to the dark*
> *And fleshed out the wonder of light*
> *And as You speak*
> *A hundred billion galaxies are born*
> *In the vapor of Your breath the planets form*
> *If the stars were made to worship so will I*
> *I can see Your heart in everything You've made*
> *Every burning star*

A signal fire of grace
If creation sings Your praises so will I.[73]

All of creation points to the Creator. Psalm 148 is one of many examples of Scripture that describes various aspects of God's creation singing or declaring praise to the Creator. What specific characteristic of God are they praising? They are praising the incredible power of the One who created them – "for at his command they were created." Their very existence points to the amazing wonder of the power of the Creator – "he issued a decree that will never pass away."

Praise the Lord.
Praise the Lord from the heavens;
praise him in the heights above.
Praise him, all his angels;
praise him, all his heavenly hosts.
Praise him, sun and moon;
praise him, all you shining stars.
Praise him, you highest heavens
and you waters above the skies.
Let them praise the name of the Lord,
for at his command they were created,
and he established them for ever and ever—
he issued a decree that will never pass away.

Psalm 148:1-6 ESV

---

[73] So Will I (100 Billion X), Words and Music by Joel Houston, Benjamin Hastings & Michael Fatkin, © 2017 Hillsong Music Publishing Australia. Used by permission.

Here's one more thought about God, our Creator. Over the years, I've tended to think of myself as a relatively creative person. I have done many things that creatives do – singing, playing cello, photography, home decorating, quilting (and all of the associated fabric collecting, which is an art, in itself), crocheting, chalk painting… But in order for me to "create" I need the equipment and the materials with which to create. The ultimate Creative, the Creator of the universe, did not gather his equipment and materials in order to create. He created out of nothing or out of chaos. Now that's creativity! We are made in his image so we are creative. But, once again, we are reminded – he is God. We are not.

Creation's post script

One of my most cherished memories of childhood adventures with my dad are the times we would stargaze. He had a star chart that rotated from the centre and matched the route of the night sky. Because we lived in Alaska, there were only a few months in the year that were ideal for stargazing and there were some months when stargazing was impossible. Summers in Alaska involve a lot of daylight. There's good reason it is called "The Land of the Midnight Sun". Therefore, the optimal months for stargazing are also the coldest months of the year. These are the darkest months.

On many-a moonlit night, my dad and I would bundle-up[74] and head outside. We'd trudge through the snow and find a great spot, away from man-made lights, and lie on our backs on that bed of snow, gazing upward. We didn't just look at the sky with a glance; we gave it our long and concerted focus. It never failed to boggle my mind. Those little dots that seemed to twinkle as their light passed through the atmosphere were celestial giants, far larger than our sun. And they were somehow suspended in space. Wowsers.

Fast forward to today. We've traded in the star charts for phone apps. Jim has an app that identifies where planets, stars and constellations are, even when they are below us on the other side of the planet. Whatever tool we use to help us identify what we're seeing, the results are still the same. Now our grandchildren are the ones to say, "Wowsers"!

When it comes to stars, we can never say that when you've seen one, you've seen them all. There are red giants, white dwarfs and main sequence stars, just to name a few. Let's consider one type of a very old star for a moment – the neutron star. These are aged relics that have collapsed into a very dense sphere. They are so dense that a mere teaspoon of a neutron star would weigh 100 million tons. Mind boggling.

On a clear night, when you are away from all city lights, you might be able to see thousands of stars. But that is really just a drop in the proverbial bucket of our universe. Within our galaxy, The Milky Way, there are between 100 and 400 billion stars. That's, at the very least, 100,000,000,000 stars. Count those zeros! That reality is completely beyond my grasp, both literally and also figuratively! I just. Don't. Get it.

Now, let's consider Genesis 1:16, "God made two great lights—the greater light to govern the day and the lesser light to govern the night. He also made the stars." Did you catch that? He also made the stars. This just makes me chuckle. Rather loudly, at times. We could spend a lifetime, as many do, studying the stars. And in the creation account, the stars are simply a tag on. A P.S. – a Post Script.

"He spreads out the northern skies over empty space;
he suspends the earth over nothing.
He wraps up the waters in his clouds,
yet the clouds do not burst under their weight.
He covers the face of the full moon,
spreading his clouds over it.
He marks out the horizon on the face of the waters
for a boundary between light and darkness."
"And these are but the outer fringe of his works;
how faint the whisper we hear of him!
Who then can understand
the thunder of his power?"
Job 26:7-10,14

Somehow, Job grasped the un-grasp-able-ness (it should be a word, don't you think?) of the power of God. After all of his poetic images for God's power at work in creation, Job says that these things are merely the "outer fringe" of God's work. They are simply faint whispers of his power.

Sustaining creation

> *"Who shut up the sea behind doors when it burst forth from the womb,*
> *when I made the clouds its garment and wrapped it in thick darkness,*
> *when I fixed limits for it and set its doors and bars in place,*
> *when I said, 'This far you may come and no farther;*
> *here is where your proud waves halt'?"*
>
> **Job 38:8-11**

God not only exercised his power in creating our world, our world is sustained by his on-going power. Yes, nature (everything made by God) takes its course, so to speak. But that course is established by the Creator and he is still the ultimate power. We'll look into this quite closely when we study the sovereignty of God. For now, let's consider one aspect of God's sustaining power – his power in holding back the seas.

> *Just before the story of the flood begins, we learn that "the Lord saw that the wickedness of man was great in the earth, and that every intention of the thoughts of his heart was only evil continually" (Genesis 6:5) and it grieved God "to his heart" (Genesis 6:6). So God sent the floodwaters as a judgment, a block in the way of humanity's wickedness that rose out of the grief of his heart (Genesis 6:5-6). Genesis describes the flood as the de-creation of the world—the earth sinks back into the chaotic waters that God cleared away on page one of the Bible (Genesis 1:6-10).*
>
> **Andy Patton**[75]

---

[75] Andy Patton, *Why Did God Flood the World*, The Bible Project, https://bibleproject.com/blog/why-did-god-flood-the-world/, posted 2019. Used by permission.

What a fascinating thought. Biblical scholars and scientists believe that, prior to the flood, our planet was surrounded by a canopy, which created misty vapor but did not allow for direct rain. When the boundaries holding the water on the earth and the water above the earth unlocked their gates, the flood occurred. I'm not a scientific or flood narrative expert so I mention this only to point out that God, in creation, brought order out of chaos. He parted the waters and the land. He created an order in the solar system, which involves a steady continuation of evenings and mornings, of days and weeks and years. When humankind's heart "was only evil continually" God simply de-created, removing his sustaining hand on the waters for a time and allowing the earth to experience unruly chaos. I'm thankful for rainbows, aren't you?![76]

Fully able

Ah, Sovereign Lord, you have made the heavens and the earth by your great power and outstretched arm. Nothing is too hard for you.
Jeremiah 32:17

No dilemma exists within God. Think about that for a moment. We, as humans, face dilemmas when two opposing forces meet. Two values we cherish may clash within us as we face an ethical dilemma. Two people may deal with a dilemma when their opposing world views collide. A husband and a wife might face a parenting dilemma when they have differing concepts of their roles in parenting. Dilemmas make life difficult. Nothing is difficult for God.

"I know that you can do all things; no purpose of yours can be thwarted."
Job 42:2

Absolutely nothing external to God can create limits on God's power. No power can come against God and, ultimately, win. Even during the challenges from Satan, he knows how the story will end. There is nothing that can make God's work more difficult to accomplish.

---

*Now to him who is able to do immeasurably more
than all we ask or imagine, according to his power that is at work within us,
to him be glory in the church and in Christ Jesus
throughout all generations, for ever and ever! Amen.*
Ephesians 3:20-21

God's power is "un-thwart-able" by evil purposes and God's power cannot even be thwarted by the way we pray. Maybe you've never had this problem but let me tell you, I have. I pray small prayers sometimes. I look at a situation in my earth-bound limitations, think through the options, consider solutions, and then present those ideas to God. Sheesh! Just putting that in print and reading it reinforces how very foolish I am! I think that I should be God's adviser? Hello! In Philippians 4:6 we are told to present our requests to God. Check it out.

> *Do not be anxious about anything, but in every situation, by prayer and petition, with thanksgiving, present your **requests** to God.*
> **Philippians 4:6, emphasis added**

Nowhere does it say to present our solutions to God. And it doesn't even say that we should present our suggestions to God. God doesn't need your advice. When we pray, what we need is to simply say – "Help me, God!" How kind of God that he lets us ramble on in our praying, at times, and then He steps in and does what he knew was best, anyway! How silly of me to, seemingly, limit God in the way I pray. Praise God for his grace as he does immeasurably more than I could ask or imagine (Ephesians 3:20-21)![77] God is not even restricted by our limited view of our situation. Nor is he restricted by our limited view of him!

Not able

So, I've tried to make it clear that God is fully able and that nothing can limit God. Then how can he also be unable? Simply this – God's limits are within himself. God cannot be, think, or do anything that is contrary to or opposing his own character. Because God is holy, he cannot sin. Because God is love, he cannot hate anything except sin. Because God is patient, he cannot be impatient with anything except sin. Because God is wise, he cannot be foolish. Because God is all-knowing, he cannot be surprised. God is unable to be anything contrary to himself.

---

[77] "Now to him who is able to do immeasurably more than all we ask or imagine, according to his power that is at work within us, to him be glory in the church and in Christ Jesus throughout all generations, for ever and ever! Amen." Ephesians 3:20-21.

> *"God is not human, that he should lie,*
> *not a human being,*
> *that he should change his mind.*
> *Does he speak and then not act?*
> *Does he promise and not fulfill?"*
>
> **Numbers 23:19**

Steady power

My dad is, as I'm writing, 92 years old. He's a feisty old Swede who has always refused to quit. That means he's taken some risks in his day... when he felt it necessary. Like the time when he had to, during a snow/wind storm in Anchorage, Alaska, cut a large tree off of the power lines so that his young family could regain power to our house. A cold winter with lots of snow and wind meant that his family needed electricity. So, he propped a ladder against the huge birch tree that had, while in mid-fall, gotten caught by the power lines. Dad climbed up the long extension of the ladder with his chainsaw in one hand and his other hand gripping the ladder rungs.

All of my questions to my mother about how she thought he'd get back down when the tree fell went unanswered. When he did cut through that mighty tree, it was able to fall off the power lines. I'll never forget that sight of my dad as the tree began to fall – there was Dad, throwing that chainsaw as far away from himself as he could even as he jumped as far as he could in the opposite direction from the trajectory of the trees and the chainsaw. I believe he just got a broken wrist out of that ordeal. Thankfully the piles of snow cushioned his fall.

Dad has been in near-death situations ten times in his adult life. He's survived four variations of cancers. He's survived severe allergic reactions to penicillin and to bee stings. He survived a misdiagnosis that landed him in Intensive Care for days and weakened his lungs for life. We're used to Dad surviving, but each health scare is still just that – a scare. I remember the time, in the mid 1990s, when Mum called to say that an ambulance was on its way to their house because Dad had been stung by a bee. We lived closer to the hospital than they did and we knew that the path the ambulance would take would be right past us so we piled the family into the car and headed over to Mum and Dad's. I was thinking that if the ambulance crew needed to stabilise Dad for any length of time, Mum would want the company. I also, deep in my sub-conscience, wanted to be there for Mum if they couldn't even get Dad to that point of stabilisation.

As we drove toward my parents' home and there was no sign of an ambulance going the other direction, I voiced into the air, for myself more than for my family – "No matter how God answers our prayers for Grandpa, God hasn't changed." You see, I knew that God had the power to heal Dad. I knew that God was fully able. And I knew that God loved this man more than any of us did. So, I trusted in God's wisdom to do what was absolutely the best for my dad.

Dad made it that day, but it took the paramedics about 30 minutes to stabilise him enough to be able to even get him into the ambulance where their work could continue. As we rounded the first curve in the road along the lake where they lived, the ambulance appeared. We turned around and made it to the hospital after Dad was all settled into a hospital room. A few hours after the whole ordeal began, one of the paramedics came out to the waiting area to update me on the situation. Her long blonde hair was matted and stiff, sticking to the sides of her face. I asked her if that was from dried sweat. It was. She said she'd never worked so long and so hard to get someone stabilised. Those paramedics saved my dad's life that day. True to form, Dad threw a party for the crew at their Fire Station after he was fully recovered. He wanted to thank them and give glory to God. Dad knew, first-hand, the kind power of God.

When I face a situation that catches me off guard, I often counsel myself by picturing God, in heaven (my own, wimpy image of such), wringing his hands and saying, "Now what are we going to do?!" Guaranteed, it always helps. Firstly, it's so silly that it lightens the moment. Secondly, it reminds me that I'm the one doing the hand-wringing. God never does such things. He never is at a loss for what to do and how best to do it. God's power is a constant. He is always all powerful. Always.

O Lord my God, when I in awesome wonder
Consider all the worlds Thy hands have made
I see the stars, I hear the rolling thunder
Thy power throughout the universe displayed
Then sings my soul, my Saviour God, to Thee
How great Thou art, how great Thou art
Then sings my soul, my Saviour God, to Thee
How great Thou art, how great Thou art!

Carl Boburg and Stuart K. Hine[78]

---

[78] Carl Boburg, *O Stura Gud*, 1885. How Great Thou Art, Stuart Wesley Keene Hine, © 1949 and 1953 Stuart Hine Trust CIO Stuart K. Hine Trust (Admin. by SHOUT! Music Publishing Australia). Used by permission.

Power restrained

In Dostoevsky's novel, **The Brothers Karamazov,**[79] Ivan Karamazov speaks of "the miracle of restraint" – that God chooses, at times, to hold back his power. This is a tremendous truth that is important to consider.

As a young girl, when I first learned about Satan tempting Jesus in the wilderness (Luke 4:3-13), I developed a strange picture in my head that has stayed with me over the many years. Satan tempts Jesus with the idea of turning some stones into bread (a very realistic temptation because Jesus had just ended a 40-day fast in the wilderness and was fully human as well as fully God so he was fully hungry). But when I read that account, I pictured Jesus, not turning stones into bread but turning Satan into a loaf of bread. My brain would see a mouth on this loaf of bread saying, "No, that's not what I meant! Help!" My access to TV was quite limited so my voracious reading led to a pretty strong imagination, I suppose! I think I enjoyed the "gotcha" feeling that accompanied such an image. Jesus could have ended Satan's temptations by ending Satan. Yet, for our sakes, for the sake of his purposes, Jesus restrained his own power. Just because he could, doesn't mean he did. Sit with that thought for a moment.

The most important place where we see God restrain his power is when it comes to our human freedom to choose. I hesitate to use the term "free will" because none of us has the power to "will" anything into existence. God's will is all-powerful; I'm hard-pressed to even will myself into resisting a beautiful slice of freshly baked (by son, Joey)

---

[79] Fyodor Dostoyevsky, *The Brothers Karamazov*, 1880.

sourdough bread with melted butter. Though I might try to "will it away" my will is rendered powerless in that situation. But I do have free choice. I could choose to walk away from that sumptuous and comfort-inducing treat.

God's incredible power could force each of us to change, to repent of our sins, to surrender to Jesus and to receive the gift he offers because of his death on the cross. But a gift, by very definition, is free and may be refused. Power, without the existence of God's other characteristics, could force us to accept the gift (which would, then, not really be a gift, after all). God's power could force us to change. Only love invites us to change.

God's terrible insistence on human freedom is so absolute
that He granted us the power to live as though He does not exist…
Why does God content Himself with the slow, unencouraging way of
making righteousness grow rather than avenging it?
That's how love is. *Love has its own power—*
the only power capable of conquering the human heart.
Philip Yancey[80]

---

[80] Philip Yancey, *The Jesus I Never Knew*, Zondervan, 1995, p. 78.

Power source

> *But he said to me, "My grace is sufficient for you,*
> *for my power is made perfect in weakness."*
> *Therefore I will boast all the more gladly about my weaknesses,*
> *so that the power of Christ may rest upon me.*
> **2 Corinthians 12:9 ESV**

Remember when I said that this character of God, his power, is one of his attributes that we cannot grow into as we become more Christlike in our nature? We definitely cannot become omnipotent. However, that doesn't mean we are hopeless in our helplessness. Hope and help are available in Jesus. In fact, the reality of our weakness points us right to the only source of power – Christ in us. I cannot boast in any power within myself. I can, however, boast in the power of God within me. Because of Jesus, I live with hope. Hallelujah!

> *I pray that out of his glorious riches he may strengthen you*
> *with power through his Spirit in your inner being.*
> **Ephesians 3:16**

We are weak. Maybe that seems offensive to you, but after all of this focus on God's power... well, you must agree. We are all pretty weak and wimpy. How very refreshing and replenishing is that truth? Truly! When I get to the place to acknowledge my weakness, there is finally hope for me. I can go to The Source. I can go to The One who does not grow tired or weary. His understanding is far beyond anything I can comprehend. When our hope is in the Lord rather than in ourselves, we can soar like eagles, run and not grow weary, walk and not even faint. Does that sound too good to be true? Have you not heard?

"To whom will you compare me?
Or who is my equal?" says the Holy One.
Lift up your eyes and look to the heavens:
Who created all these?
He who brings out the starry host one by one
and calls forth each of them by name.
Because of his great power and mighty strength,
not one of them is missing.
Do you not know?
Have you not heard?
The Lord is the everlasting God,
the Creator of the ends of the earth.
He will not grow tired or weary,
and his understanding no one can fathom.
He gives strength to the weary
and increases the power of the weak.
Even youths grow tired and weary,
and young men stumble and fall;
but those who hope in the Lord
will renew their strength.
They will soar on wings like eagles;
they will run and not grow weary,
they will walk and not be faint.

Isaiah 40:25-26; 28-31

For Reflection

1. On the next available clear night, do some stargazing of your own or invite a friend to join you. And if the city lights or clouds limit your options, do an internet search for the Hubble Ultra-Deep Field. Gaze. Keep gazing. Respond to the Creator.

2. Set aside some time to look back at your past ten years. Where have you seen God's power at work in your life and in the lives of people around you? You could list the ways. Then thank God for his power.

3. Have you been trying, in small or large ways, to limit God's power in your life by praying suggestions instead of requests? Because God knows that about you already, you might as well just "'fess up"! Thank God for his kindness in not going with the limits you set. Ask the Holy Spirit to transform the way you pray so that you can just pray thanks and requests and leave the solutions to God.

4. Where are you feeling weak at the moment? Set aside time right now to sit at the feet, so to speak, of The One who is your source. If you can't do it immediately, at least schedule a time to do it this week. Just sit. In silence. If you're done offering your advice to God, silence is really a great next step!

12

GOD IS ALL-KNOWING AND ALL-WISE

To say that God is omniscient is to say that He possesses perfect knowledge and therefore has no need to learn. But it is more; it is to say that God has never learned and cannot learn.

A.W. Tozer[81]

Just now, I relocated my laptop and other gear to our dining room table for a change of scenery. (We'll see if I can withstand the distraction of the rolling hills beyond the large sliding glass doors.) Looking up one last time as I prepared to resume writing, I had a realisation. It hit me that, after un-decorating the house from Christmas, we had not put a particularly large duck-egg-blue bowl back above the kitchen cabinets. (We: a proverbial term because with a husband who is just under 6'8" I rarely grab a stepladder. Usually, I just wait for him to reappear.)

You and I have realisations throughout our day. We might realise that we forgot to eat lunch. We might realise, the hard way, that we forgot to put fuel in our car. Not so with God. God. Never. Realises.

[81] A.W. Tozer, *The Knowledge of the Holy*, Harper & Row, 1961, 1975 edition, p. 61.

Anything. He has no "a-ha" moments. He never figures something out. He never discovers something new. Never.

So, with that realisation, let's dig into two aspects of God's understanding. He is not only all-knowing (omniscient: omni = all; science = knowing), he is also all-wise. God knows everything that has happened and is happening. God knows everything that could happen. That means that he knows every possibility and, more importantly, he knows which option is best. He sees it all, he understands it all, he knows the implications of it all. He knows every minute detail of everything that he knows. His knowledge is that complete. In Matthew 10:30,[82] we read that the hairs on our heads are numbered.

The point is that God knows the number of hairs on your head not because He counted them, but because He is God and He knows. All of the information in all the libraries of the world; all the data on all the computer chips in the world, including the K-wave quantum computers and those that have not yet been made; all of this data, God knows perfectly and completely right now.

Tony Evans[83]

Know-how

My dad is brilliant. He has a PhD as well and other degrees, always repaired his own vehicles, built the houses we lived in, and he never called a repairman for anything. My dad is a man with a lot of know-how. Maybe it's an old-fashioned term, know-how. It's used to describe someone who has skills

---

[82] "And even the very hairs of your head are all numbered." Matthew 10:30.
[83] Tony Evans, *God Himself: A Journey through His Attributes*, Moody Publishers, 2020, p. 35. Used by permission.

and uses those skills well such as a handy man/woman who is both knowledgeable and skilled. In my mind, I can hear my dad say "know-how", but I'm not sure I've heard the word from anyone else in recent years. Growing up with my dad as my standard of measurement, I suppose Jim had a bit of pressure on him when we first married. Jim is, indeed, a man of know-how. (Really, how could I choose otherwise?!) I say, rather often, "Honey, I have an idea." He knows there's work ahead; a project is in his future. Jim actually is happiest when doing projects; he's built homes, remodelled homes, learned the art of landscaping... you name it. In our current home in the wooded hills above the city of Gold Coast, when I suggest something that we could do to change the supporting wall of gardens alongside the swimming pool, he says, "I KNOW HOW we could do that." But just this morning, when he saw that the pool pump was drawing in air, he said, "I don't know how... I need to check it out."

You see, Jim is a man of know-how, but sometimes he needs to learn how. God is truly our God of know-how. Think about that phrase for a moment. God knows: he knows all that there is to know past, present, future. He also fully contains the "how". He knows what is best and he knows how to accomplish what is best. Maybe "know-how" is the best way to explain that God is both all-knowing and all-wise.

Wisdom... is the ability to devise perfect ends and to achieve those ends by the most perfect means. It sees the end from the beginning, so there can be no need to guess or conjecture.
A.W. Tozer[84]

---

[84] A.W. Tozer, *The Knowledge of the Holy*, Harper & Row, 1961, 1975 edition, p. 66.

What can we tell God?

So, why do we pray? If God knows everything, why do we need to talk with him? When I meet with someone who is in a dilemma of some sort, after we've talked through the situation – the feelings, and all related issues – after we've considered God's Word and after we've thought through a Biblical view of the situation, after all of our talking is done… I will say, "Could we pray?" (Of course, I've been praying in my head all along – a whole lot of "help me, God" prayers!) And as I pray for this one person and their needs, I often begin by saying, "Thank you, Lord, that we don't have to catch you up on our conversation. Thank you that we don't need to fill you in on some facts. So, here's this whole messy thing, God. I lift it up to you and say 'Help!'"

What a joy and privilege is ours when we pray. We don't have to give God the facts, we don't need to advise him in any way, we don't need to suggest solutions. We can pray for breakthrough, wisdom, insight, courage, new strength. We can pray for peace "in the midst" – in the midst of the stress, in the midst of the uncertainty, in the midst of the waiting. But one thing we never have to do when we pray is to get God up to speed. That reality might actually wipe out a lot of our praying. And it just might get us praying for the really important pieces! God doesn't need you to pray so that he knows what's going on in your life. WE need to pray. Prayer changes things. Others are changed when we pray for them. We are changed when we pray for others and for ourselves.

When I used to teach English as a Second Language, I would try to explain the difference between "talk to" and "talk with" because those little prepositions matter. Body language helped in the explanation.

For "talk to" I stood, facing a student directly, and I might wag a finger at them as I'm telling them what they need to do. For "talk with" I sat next to them, at a slight angle so that I could see them but still be alongside them. Does that make sense? When someone says, "Sharon, I need to talk to you!" I think, "Oh-oh!" and when someone says, "Sharon, I want to talk with you!" I think, "How lovely!" Can you see the difference? Let's not forget that prayer is talking WITH our God. It is intimate. It is relational. It is two-way. Sometimes, when we pray, we sit in silence. It's tough to hear an answer when we're filibustering, after all.

Questioning

Have you ever noticed how often God asks questions? (Did you notice what I just did there?) As a teacher, I ask questions of students for many different reasons. The various reasons have the same underlying reason, though. Always, I ask questions in order for someone to learn something. Sometimes I ask questions because I want to draw out a student. Sometimes I ask a question because I want to start a discussion. Rarely do I ask a question that has only one right answer. That would be done only when we're reviewing content or "take aways" from a lecture and even then, there probably wouldn't be only one right answer. In a discussion, sometimes I ask questions because I am the one who needs to learn. I want to learn their background, their worldview, their values... I want to get to know the student so that I can more effectively impact them. And, in that discussion, I am hoping the student, or students, learn more about themselves, too.

God never asks us questions in order to get to know us. There's no small talk with God, hallelujah! But God does ask questions. We see it in the

Old Testament as God interacted with humankind. We see it in the New Testament with Jesus and the people he encountered. We see it hundreds of times throughout Scripture. Here are a few examples. As you read each question, consider the reasons God is asking the question.

Then the man and his wife heard the sound of the Lord God as he was walking in the garden in the cool of the day, and they hid from the Lord God among the trees of the garden. But the Lord God called to the man, "Where are you?"

Genesis 3:8-9

Moses answered, "What if they do not believe me or listen to me and say, 'The Lord did not appear to you'?" Then the Lord said to him, "What is that in your hand?" "A staff," he replied.

Exodus 4:1-2

"Where were you when I laid the earth's foundation? Tell me, if you understand."

Job 38:4

"Why do you look at the speck of sawdust in your brother's eye and pay no attention to the plank in your own eye?"

Matthew 7:3

"But what about you?" he asked. "Who do you say I am?"

Matthew 16:15

Jesus stopped and called them. "What do you want me to do for you?" he asked.

Matthew 20:32

God is never the one who has something to learn from his questions. We are the ones. With great intentionality, God asks questions to prove a point – "Where are you?" "Where were you when I …?" And he asks questions to introduce an idea – "What is in your hand?" And he asks questions to get us to think about what we believe – "Who do you say …?" And he asks questions to get us to be honest with him – "What do you want …?" These are just a few examples; there are many more reasons and a vast array of questions to be found in our Bible. Wouldn't it be a fascinating study – the questions God asks of us?

I love watching our daughter, Jeri, parent her kids. When one of them cries from another room, she calmly-but-swiftly goes to them and asks, "Are you crying because you're scared or because you're hurt?" How brilliant! Without the knowledge she would have had, had she been right there, she needs to quickly assess if there is an injury, which requires immediate attention, or if there's a soul that needs some care. God doesn't need to ask us. He hears our cries before we even cry. And he stands ready with an answer to our every need.

Who can fathom the Spirit of the Lord,
or instruct the Lord as his counselor?
Whom did the Lord consult to enlighten him,
and who taught him the right way?
Who was it that taught him knowledge,
or showed him the path of understanding?

Isaiah 40:13-14

The wisdom of the Gospel

All that God does is perfectly wise and is done with full knowledge of all possibilities. The best example of this is seen in the Gospel (meaning: Good News). I cannot fully grasp the Gospel, the Good News of Jesus. But I can know that it is true. God had to become one of us so that he could die for all of us. Maybe it is the very thought of such perfect wisdom found in the Good News of Jesus that proves it to be true. No human could conceive of such a solution for our sin. We might try to hide our sin, excuse our sin, pay for our sin. Each effort would end in failure.

Only at the cross do we see the perfect solution. At the cross where Jesus died, the righteousness of God that demands justice meets the love of God that demands grace. The Gospel combines the three essentials of the message of good news: the incarnation of Christ Jesus, the death of Jesus to pay the penalty for the sins of anyone who chooses to surrender ownership of their life to him, and the resurrection of this spotless Lamb who reigns forever as our King. This is the Good News. This is the Gospel. Such profound wisdom is found there.

The beginning of wisdom

> *In all this you greatly rejoice, though now for a little while you may have had to suffer grief in all kinds of trials. These have come so that the proven genuineness of your faith— of greater worth than gold, which perishes even though refined by fire— may result in praise, glory and honor when Jesus Christ is revealed.*
>
> **1 Peter 1:6-7**

Notice what is NOT being tested, here – wisdom. We don't need to have the answers in order to "pass the test"! People who don't seek the wisdom of the Holy Spirit have to fall back on their own wisdom in times of stress. They have to try their best to reason their way out of it. I've had friends say that they just need to get through their situation because it will make them stronger, wiser, better. True, we can, most certainly, grow through a trial; we can become wiser and avoid a similar trial in the future. But, for followers of Jesus, that is not the main result of the struggle. Struggles increase our faith in the One who is our source. God is our go-to for everything that comes our way. As our faith grows, we increasingly know this to be absolutely true.

James, in the letter he wrote to the Jewish people who were scattered by conquerors, speaks of the very same idea that we find in Peter's letter, above. It is our faith that is tested during times of strife. After talking about persevering through trials with faith, James says that there is something simple to do when we lack wisdom, as we surely will. We simply need to ask God for it.

If any of you lacks wisdom, you should ask God, who gives generously to all without finding fault, and it will be given to you. But when you ask, you must believe and not doubt, because the one who doubts is like a wave of the sea, blown and tossed by the wind. That person should not expect to receive anything from the Lord. Such a person is double-minded and unstable in all they do.

James 1:5-8

Notice that James says that we should not doubt. This doubt seems to speak to divided loyalty. Could it be that we ask God for wisdom and then still seek wisdom from an ungodly source? Perhaps you, like me, have asked God for wisdom and when he has said, "Be still," you have gone off and tried to solve things on your own. Being still just seems so unproductive, we rationalise. Here, the promise is clear. If we need wisdom and ask God for it, he will gladly give it to us, without even scolding us! We simply need to have an undivided heart in our response. As the old saying goes – "Says easy. Does hard." Maybe the following reminder can help us. It's all of these aspects packed into one verse – wisdom, knowledge and understanding. All are found in the Lord.

The fear of the Lord is the beginning of wisdom, and knowledge of the Holy One is understanding.

Proverbs 9:10

No need to hide

You have searched me, Lord, and you know me.
You know when I sit and when I rise;
you perceive my thoughts from afar.
You discern my going out and my lying down;
you are familiar with all my ways.
Before a word is on my tongue
you, Lord, know it completely.

Psalm 139:1-4

> *Nothing in all creation is hidden from God's sight. Everything is uncovered and laid bare before the eyes of him to whom we must give account.*
> **Hebrews 4:13**

Because God is all-knowing, there is no need to even try to hide anything from him. We can, as I've said before, bring to him what IS in us, not what OUGHT to be in us. Though the writer to the Hebrews says, as seen above, that everything is laid bare and we must give an account, I do not find this reality disconcerting. Remember this – God knows that deep down, in the corner of your heart, you want to obey him. And he knows when you can't get that far and you simply want to want to obey him. God knows our thoughts even before we think them. Astounding. Comforting. He knows me better than I know myself and he loves me. Still.

So, there's no reason to hide. What's the point? And if God knows and sees all actions and thoughts, which he does, then I can admit my guilt and find forgiveness. Every time. And I can surrender, again, and ask the Holy Spirit to take control of my thoughts and my deeds. I can ask him to enable me to do the things I am able to do that will permit him to do the things I can't do.

The beyond of God

We have a grandson who is in the questioning stage in a big way. His questions astound me, though, because he's only four years old. He asks "what happens if" questions. "Mummy, what happens if a man doesn't have a house to live in?" "Mummy, what happens if it doesn't rain?" "Mummy, what happens if the moon explodes?" "Mummy, what happens if ..." You see the trend. His mummy does her best to answer every question in a concrete way. But some things cannot be comprehended. They are beyond us. Yet, get this – God knows every answer to every "what happens if" question for all time. Here is but one example in the teachings of Jesus.

"Woe to you, Chorazin! Woe to you, Bethsaida!
For if the miracles that were performed in you had been performed
in Tyre and Sidon, they would have repented long ago in sackcloth and ashes."
Matthew 11:21

God's knowledge and wisdom is so far beyond ours that I wish there were different words we could use in order to distinguish our knowledge and wisdom from the knowledge and wisdom of God. I guess that's where "omni" (meaning "all") comes in. I looked up ideas for an antonym of the prefix "omni". The prefix options include: "nought", "non", "im", "in". But as humans, made in the image of our Creator, we do have some wisdom and knowledge. And we can grow in our wisdom and knowledge. So maybe the best prefix for us would be "mini". God is omniscient; you and I are mini-scient. Okay, it's not really a word, but it makes some sense, right? God's wisdom and knowledge transcend all of our combined wisdom and knowledge. This is one of the "beyonds" of God.

> *Oh, the depth of the riches of the wisdom and knowledge of God!*
> *How unsearchable his judgments,*
> *and his paths beyond tracing out!*
> *"Who has known the mind of the Lord?*
> *Or who has been his counselor?"*
> *"Who has ever given to God,*
> *that God should repay them?"*
> *For from him and through him and*
> *for him are all things.*
> *To him be the glory forever! Amen.*
>
> **Romans 11:33-36**

We used the above verses as a key focus in our wedding. True, these are not typical wedding verses. We simply wanted the focus of our wedding... and our lives... to be on God. From him and through him and for him are all things. I love the way this Doxology begins – the wisdom and knowledge of God are deep riches. His judgements are unsearchable and his paths cannot be understood. I hear some of you saying, "Amen!" In those times when you cannot see, you can trust the only One who fully sees.

For Reflection

1. Spend some good time considering and writing about the following: God's knowledge and wisdom in creation; God's knowledge and wisdom in salvation; God's knowledge and wisdom with each individual; God's knowledge and wisdom in your own life. Share your discoveries with someone!

2. Think about the ways you've prayed, lately. Have you tried to fill God in on the facts? Have you advised God in any way? Now, go to God in prayer, confessing any way that you might have come to him as though he needed your wisdom and insight. Talk with him about your fears, your sense of powerlessness. Ask him to do a mighty work within you – bringing clarity, wisdom, patience… peace.

3. Hang out in the book of Proverbs for a while. Notice all of the mention of wisdom and the wisdom that is required to pursue wisdom.

4. Read James 1:5. Talk with God about an area in which you need God's wisdom, today. Thank him for his unlimited supply of wisdom and knowledge.

13

GOD IS EVERYWHERE-PRESENT

God is over all things; under all things; outside all; within but not enclosed; without but not excluded; above but not raised up; below but not depressed; wholly above, presiding; wholly beneath, sustaining; wholly within, filling.

Hildebert of Lavardin[85]

That God is everywhere present means that God is here. He is in your here even as he is in my here; he is in your here that is my there, my here that is your tomorrow. He is here when I'm writing this. He is here when you are reading this. He is present. Always and everywhere. God is not limited by time. God is not limited by space.

In the psalm, below, we see the word "very". This word can be translated greatly, extremely, strongly. It is a well-proven truth. God is extremely present in our lives. And, more importantly for our daily lives, he is our helpful presence. He is here. He is our help.

---

[85] Hildebert of Lavardin, Bishop of Le Mans and Archbishop of Tours, 1055-1133 AD.

> *God is our refuge and strength, a very present help in trouble.*
> **Psalm 46:1 ESV**

Rotations and revolutions

As a function of the earth's rotation on its axis, we have roughly 24 hours in our day. As a function of the earth's revolution around the sun, we have roughly 365 days in a year. It is within these constraints that we live. That is all we know. As soon as we snap our fingers, the snap that is part of the present becomes part of the past. We are so very limited within the timeline created by rotations and revolutions. Is it any wonder, then, that we struggle with grasping that God is in our yesterday and our today and our tomorrow… all right now? Once again, we are confronted with the beyond of God.

Because we, in Australia, are 19 hours ahead of our family and friends in Alaska, I can tell them how great their tomorrow is. For me, it's an "is". For them it's a "will be". And I'll never forget when my brother's wife gave birth to a baby on a continent in a much earlier time zone than Alaska. My father was proudly telling everyone he saw, "I had a new granddaughter born tomorrow." Our language speaks of yesterday, today, tomorrow… before and after. When we mess with it, it's confusing. Our language uses linear terms. We measure where we've been and where we are going. We even have boundaries to delineate time – time zones, international date lines, daylight savings. We live our lives on a continuum – birth, toddlerhood, pre-school, primary school, high school, university, post-graduate, middle aged, elderly. It actually seems reasonable that we struggle with comprehending a God who already is in our tomorrow at the same time he is in our yesterday.

We must remember that our "time" is a function of the creation that was designed by the Creator. And, as we've said before, he lives beyond the boundaries of creation. The following verse indicates this truth so well. When we wait. And wait. And wait for God to move in some way, how comforting it is to remember that he is not bound by our understanding of time. When he moves, what he does happens quickly.

"I am the Lord; in its time I will do this swiftly."
Isaiah 60:22b

Here and there

Maybe because of time travel movies and because of books by Madeleine L'Engle we are able to, ever-so-slightly, grasp the out-of-the-box idea of moving through time. But those fantasies will never help us understand being in every point in time at the same time. Another toughie to understand is this – God is everywhere in space at the same time. God is right here and over there… right now. Every part of the Trinity is involved. The Father is everywhere present, the Son is Immanuel – God with us, and the Spirit is within every believer.

David wrestled with this truth in Psalm 139.

> *Where can I go from your Spirit?*
> *Where can I flee from your presence?*
> *If I go up to the heavens, you are there;*
> *if I make my bed in the depths, you are there.*
> *If I rise on the wings of the dawn,*
> *if I settle on the far side of the sea,*
> *even there your hand will guide me,*
> *your right hand will hold me fast.*
> *If I say, "Surely the darkness will hide me*
> *and the light become night around me,"*
> *even the darkness will not be dark to you;*
> *the night will shine like the day,*
> *for darkness is as light to you.*
>
> **Psalm 139:7-12**

Some might see this as a bit of a good news/bad news situation. God is right there, everywhere. Great. God is right there, everywhere. Oh dear – not so great. Maybe it's a comforting reality for you – God hears you when you call to him. He is your constant companion. Maybe there's no comfort, here, at all – you'd rather go to church to meet with him and then leave him at church in order to get on with your plans. Well, if you've decided to join the adventure and truly embrace all of the other attributes of God – his patience with you, his compassion for you, his loyal love toward you, his mercy and grace that is available to you... maybe then you'll find delight in knowing that God is always there. It's nothing to fear... only embrace it!

> *The knowledge that we are never alone calms the troubled sea*
> *of our lives and speaks peace to our souls.*
> **A.W. Tozer**[86]

Never alone

Ron Mehl, in his gut-honest book, **God Works the Night Shift**, tells the story of a father and daughter who returned to an empty house after burying their wife/mother. The father set up his daughter's little bed in his room so that they could face the night together. After hours of struggling and failing to sleep, this father's heart was completely overwhelmed by the ongoing sobs of his little girl as she cried for her mother. I'll let Ron Mehl tell more of the story.

> *Thinking his daughter was asleep, the father looked up and said brokenly,*
> *"I trust you, Father, but... it's as dark as midnight!"*
> *Hearing her dad's prayer, the little girl began to cry again.*
> *"Papa, did you ever know it could be so dark?*
> *Why Papa, I can't even see you, it's so dark."*
> *Then through her tears, the little girl whispered, "But you love me even if it's dark, don't you, Papa? You love me even if I don't see you, don't you, Papa?"*[87]

The reality that God is everywhere means that God is with us. Even when it's dark. Even when we can't see him. God is with us and God is faithful.

Incline and hear

Earlier, I mentioned that Jim and I led a mid-week pre-school kids' program when our own children were young. Many were surprised that this giant of a man, all 6'8" of him, could be effective with pre-school children. Wouldn't they be intimidated and fearful of him? Well, firstly, my husband's nickname long ago with his oilfield peers was Gentle Giant. He has always been as gentle as he is tall. So, for those pre-schoolers, that helped reduce fears, to be sure. But the key to his success was when he realised that, to be effective with these little people, they'd need to see more than his knees. So, he always bent down toward them, often getting down on one knee. He **inclined** himself toward them. This is the picture the Hebrew word, translated below, carries – someone who is much bigger than us who is bending down (inclining) toward us.

I waited patiently for the Lord;
he inclined to me and heard my cry.
Psalm 40:1 ESV

Notice in the above verse that God not only bends toward us but he hears. Of course, we learned in the previous chapter that God hears our cries even before we cry them. But the picture in this verse addresses the reality of his presence. He is near enough to hear (in human terms, of course). And in this case, "hearing" means something like actually listening.

When we lived in Saudi Arabia, we HEARD live, in-person, Islamic prayers being prayed five times per day. Because the prayer times change with the cycles of the moon and sun, we even had apps on our phones that gave us the up-to-date times for each prayer. (During prayers, all commerce stopped. Shops had to close. This could be a real goal-blocker if one had errands to run.) We definitely heard the prayers. In our compound, we could hear unique prayers from two different mosques that were just beyond our cement compound walls. Imagine the distress when the imams were singing in incompatible keys from each other. Yes, we heard them. If we understood Arabic, we might have tried to listen. We HEARD but did not LISTEN. This is never true of God! He hears, he listens, he responds and he acts (according to what is best). That can only happen if he is there. And he always is.

I sought the Lord, and he answered me;
he delivered me from all my fears.

Psalm 34:4

I love the Lord, for he heard my voice;
he heard my cry for mercy.
Because he turned his ear to me,
I will call on him as long as I live.

Psalm 116:1-2

For Reflection

1. Consider the name Immanuel – God with us. Search online for some lyrics that are about that name. I'll suggest one, which is jam-packed with the concept of Immanuel without using that name: ***Arrival***, by Hillsong Worship.[88] One line captured my imagination so much that I painted some old, weathered boards with the lyrics: "Royalty robed in the flesh he created"!

---

[88] Michael Chislett, Benjamin Hastings, Matthew Crocker, Dylan Thomas, *Arrival*, Hillsong Worship, 2017.

Mind boggling. Go ahead, let your mind be boggled.

2. What comforts you about God being everywhere-present? What distresses you about it? Talk with God…

3. God is here. Consider what you can do to become more aware of God's presence in your days and minutes. Maybe you could set a Pause Goal of three times per day to help you become more aware that God is there. Stop. Sit. Sit it in the presence of God.

4. Brother Lawrence was a 17th century French lay monk with a fully devoted heart for God. Below are a few of his statements. Prayerfully consider each one.

But this King, filled with goodness and mercy, far from chastising me, lovingly embraces me, makes me eat at His table, serves me with His own hands, gives me the keys of His treasures and treats me as His favorite. He talks with me and is delighted with me in a thousand and one ways; He forgives me and relieves me of my principle bad habits without talking about them; I beg Him to make me according to His heart and always the more weak and despicable I see myself to be, the more beloved I am of God.

I cannot imagine how religious persons can live satisfied without the practice of the presence of GOD. For my part I keep myself retired with Him in the depth of centre of my soul as much as I can; and while I am so with Him I fear nothing; but the least turning from Him is insupportable.

That we should establish ourselves in a sense of GOD's Presence, by continually conversing with Him. That it was a shameful thing to quit His conversation, to think of trifles and fooleries.[89]

14
GOD IS SOVEREIGN

"With whom will you compare me or count me equal?
To whom will you liken me that we may be compared?"

"Remember the former things, those of long ago;
I am God, and there is no other;
I am God, and there is none like me.
I make known the end from the beginning,
from ancient times, what is still to come.
I say, 'My purpose will stand,
and I will do all that I please.'
From the east I summon a bird of prey;
from a far-off land, a man to fulfill my purpose.
What I have said, that I will bring about;
what I have planned, that I will do.
Listen to me, you stubborn-hearted,
you who are now far from my righteousness.
I am bringing my righteousness near,
it is not far away;
and my salvation will not be delayed.
I will grant salvation to Zion,
my splendor to Israel."

Isaiah 46:5, 9-13

Before we begin this topic on God's sovereignty, breathe deeply. Inhale… two… three, exhale… two… three. It's a tough topic.

For as long as I can remember, this attribute of God has been my favourite. It has brought me the greatest comfort and reassurance in tough times. I can hear the voice of my son, Brad, over the many years, "I know, Mum. Now you're going to mention that God is sovereign." I suppose it was a consistent theme of conversation as our kids were growing up. Whenever we hit a roadblock on our journey, whenever disappointment came our way, whenever we were frustrated by unreached goals – I would say how glad I was to know, with confidence, that God is sovereign. Sometimes, a child (or all three) would groan a bit when I'd say such a thing. They were glad I felt comforted, I suppose, but the reminder of God's sovereignty didn't take away the sting of defeat. Truly, for many, God's sovereignty is the most troubling aspect of God's character.

Does God control everything in our lives? Does he direct the sunrise each morning? Does he guide the tides of the world's oceans? Does he give you the best parking spot in the car park? If he does control everything then why is there famine on the continent of Africa? Why does a pandemic sweep across the globe? Why is there enormous drought and why is it often followed by severe fires? And why does the rain always seem to come AFTER the fires so that overwhelming flooding results? Why do evil despots prosper? Why is there social injustice? Why are some people underprivileged simply because of the place they were born or the colour of their skin or both? If God... then why...?

Obviously, the above questions cannot be answered, fully, in one chapter of one book. These are dilemmas that still remain after rigorous debates over the centuries. Some church denominations began because of their answers to such questions. Often the one thing that separates one group of Christians from another are those very answers. But we cannot avoid this important attribute of God simply because it can get messy. So, let's get going!

A definition

Dictionaries speak of "sovereign" as a description of someone who has ultimate authority, is the highest power and is completely independent. The word originates from the Latin word, which means "above, over". The word, therefore, refers to a person who reigns over others.

> "Ah, Sovereign Lord, you have made the heavens and the earth
> by your great power and outstretched arm. Nothing is too hard for you."
> **Jeremiah 32:17**

> "Ah, Lord God! It is you who have made the heavens and the earth by your great power and by your outstretched arm! Nothing is too hard for you."
> **Jeremiah 32:17 ESV**

> "Dear God, my Master, you created earth and sky by your great power—
> by merely stretching out your arm! There is nothing you can't do."
> **Jeremiah 32:17 MSG**

In the three translations of Jeremiah 32:17, above, we see the difficulty that arises when trying to communicate that God is the Supreme Ruler. Two Hebrew names for God are used together. The second Hebrew word is God's title, **Yahweh**, the proper name of the God of

Israel, the name that traditionally was unspoken and unwritten out of reverence for him. This is usually translated "God" or "Lord" (with small caps) in our Bibles. The name for God that precedes **Yahweh,** in this verse, is **Adonai**. It is usually translated "Lord" (with no small caps). This word reinforces the idea that God is Master, or Lord, over all of us. In the Old Testament, the name **Adonai** is occasionally used for other beings, either human or angelic. In those cases, also, it refers to someone who "lords over" another or others. It is someone who has leadership power.

Another name for God, and the Hebrew word most commonly translated "God" or "god" (for "small g" gods), is **El** (the singular form) or **Elohim** (the plural form). It carries the idea of strength and power. Together, these three names, which are most often used for God, make it quite clear that he has authority and power to rule.

Nebuchadnezzar then approached the opening of the blazing furnace and shouted, "Shadrach, Meshach and Abednego, servants of the Most High God, come out! Come here!" So Shadrach, Meshach and Abednego came out of the fire.
Daniel 3:26

And here we have an additional name for God, **El-Elyon**, which is best translated "the Most High God" or "God Most High". **El,** which is used by Israel and the nations surrounding Israel for both God and "small-g" gods, is combined with the word rendered "most high" in order to communicate that God is above all gods. Interestingly, this word is often the name for God that is used by foreign, Gentile rulers when they are speaking of the God of Israel. This is the case with King Nebuchadnezzar in the Daniel passage, above. That's a profound thought to consider – that these kings who worshipped and feared a variety of gods, all of the "small-g" sort, acknowledged that the God of Israel was the God who is MOST high.

The independence of God

His sovereignty requires that He be absolutely free, which means simply that He must be free to do whatever He wills to do anywhere at any time to carry out His eternal purpose in every single detail without interference. Were He less than free He must be less than sovereign.
A.W. Tozer[90]

Tozer explains, in his book, ***The Knowledge of the Holy,*** that the reason this truth is so difficult to grasp is that we live in a world in which there is no example of unqualified freedom. Every creature is dependent upon other creatures and/or other elements of creation. Even a harsh dictator who wields deadly power has no power over the weather and, in reality, no power over his own length of life.

In his freedom, God cannot be hindered from doing anything. He cannot be forced against his will to do something, nor can he be stopped from doing whatever he determines to do. God is free of all constraints. God is supremely "other". He is over all that he has made and is distinctly different from all that has been made.

[90] A.W. Tozer, *The Knowledge of the Holy,* Harper & Row, 1961, 1975 edition, p. 115.

As we've discussed previously, God is beyond us in so many ways that we have, in our finite minds, a difficult time grasping descriptions of him. Lacking any illustrations around us, we can simply acknowledge that only God is fully independent, whether we can grasp it or not.

> *"I know that you can do all things;*
> *no purpose of yours can be thwarted."*
> **Job 42:2**

The authority of God

> *To whom would God go for permission?*
> *Who is higher than the Highest? Who is*
> *mightier than the Almighty? Whose position*
> *antedates that of the Eternal? At whose throne*
> *would God kneel? Where is the greater one*
> *to whom He must appeal?*
> **A.W. Tozer**[91]

God's sovereignty involves both might and right. Not only does God have complete power to do whatever he pleases (might) but he has complete authority to do whatever he pleases (right). This means that he has no higher power that he must consult. No one has more

---

[91] Ibid. p. 116.

authority than God. The whole earth is his. As Creator of the universe, he has the right to do whatever he chooses and whatever he chooses is always right.

Then King David went in and sat before the Lord, and he said: "Who am I, Sovereign Lord, and what is my family, that you have brought me this far? And as if this were not enough in your sight, Sovereign Lord, you have also spoken about the future of the house of your servant— and this decree, Sovereign Lord, is for a mere human! What more can David say to you? For you know your servant, Sovereign Lord. For the sake of your word and according to your will, you have done this great thing and made it known to your servant. How great you are, Sovereign Lord! There is no one like you and there is no God but you, as we have heard with our own ears."

2 Samuel 7:18-22

Just as in Jeremiah 32:17, in the above verses we see two of the Hebrew words for God, **Adonai Yahweh**, translated "Sovereign Lord". David is declaring that there is no one like **Adonai Yahweh;** God's authority is so supreme that, even in a world accustomed to having many gods and spiritual beings with power, God is like no other. His authority is unmatched. David could admit that his own successes were, actually, not his own at all for it was God who brought him that far.

The responsibility of humanity

There are two parallel truths to consider. I believe they are more compatible than it might seem at first glance. God has authority, as mentioned above, AND humanity has responsibility. We find two major ways in which we have responsibility – as image-bearers of the Most High God and as those given the charge to rule over the earth. We see both, below.

Then God said, "Let us make mankind in our image, in our likeness, so that they may rule over the fish in the sea and the birds in the sky, over the livestock and all the wild animals, and over all the creatures that move along the ground."
Genesis 1:26

The Lord God took the man and put him in the Garden of Eden to work it and take care of it. Now the Lord God had formed out of the ground all the wild animals and all the birds in the sky. He brought them to the man to see what he would name them; and whatever the man called each living creature, that was its name. So the man gave names to all the livestock, the birds in the sky and all the wild animals.
Genesis 2:15,19-20a

So, humankind has been given immense freedom within the context of that responsibility – to rule over all that God created. It appears that God didn't even give input on the naming of every animal. (If I was God, by the way, I'd surely want to have input. Aardvark, really?) This is the first example of the role of "stewards" – those who are given charge of another's property. We, as a part of humanity, are tasked with stewarding God's creation. That's quite a lot of freedom, it seems. And responsibility.

With responsibility comes the acceptance of consequences. When we look over the history of humanity, we see many times that humankind has suffered, not from punishment at the hand of God but from a natural consequence of humanity's failings and shortcomings. Which leads us to the next thought...

The tough questions

You might have been reading this chapter with some lingering, "Yes, but..." questions. Most of those questions can be grouped into two categories – evil and free choice. So, we need to consider the origin, existence, and apparent free rein that evil has on earth and then we need to consider humanity's free choice and how that coexists with God's control.

> *Just because God is faithful does not mean that everything is going to go perfectly. Chapters 4 and 5 [of Lamentations] vividly describe the suffering of the people of Jerusalem.*
> *Sovereignty does not eliminate calamity, and Jeremiah is fully aware of that. The writer realizes that the people deserve the judgement they are facing (4:13), but he also knows that God is in control over everything both good and bad (3:37). Therefore, the book ends with a humble plea as the writer recognized the sovereign rule of God and begged that he not ignore the cries of his people.*
> **The Jesus Bible**[92]

The problem of evil

Certainly, we all agree that evil is problematic, in itself. Even though each of us sin, most of us would state that we hate evil. We would all prefer to live in a world without evil. Foundationally, evil is a problem for us because we are unsure of its origin and we question why God allows it to exist. Here's what we know:

God hates sin.

The wrath of God is being revealed from heaven against all the godlessness and wickedness of people, who suppress the truth by their wickedness. – **Romans 1:18**

God cannot sin.

For you are not a God who delights in wickedness; evil may not dwell with you. – **Psalm 5:4 ESV**

This is the message we have heard from him and proclaim to you, that God is light, and in him is no darkness at all. – **1 John 1:5 ESV**

God is not the source of evil.

Let no one say when he is tempted, "I am being tempted by God," for God cannot be tempted with evil, and he himself tempts no one. But each person is tempted when he is lured and enticed by his own desire. Then desire when it has conceived gives birth to sin, and sin when it is fully grown brings forth death. – **James 1:13-15 ESV**

Humanity is responsible when we choose evil. God's purposes are accomplished, even through wicked agents.

This man was handed over to you by God's deliberate plan and foreknowledge; and you, with the help of wicked men, put him to death by nailing him to the cross. – **Acts 2:23**

God ultimately overrules evil.

You intended to harm me, but God intended it for good to accomplish what is now being done, the saving of many lives. – **Genesis 50:20**

There are some very positive results that come from identifying evil. Light appears brighter in the darkness. The great contrast between all that is good and all that is evil is obvious. Just as darkness is the absence of light so evil is the absence of goodness. (See the chapter entitled God is Good.) God's love and grace and mercy and compassion and patience and kindness – all that is good – becomes so much easier to see, so much easier to embrace, and so much easier to receive when it is contrasted to evil.

This line of reasoning leads us on to the next great question. Do we have free choice and, if so, why do we? Love doesn't force us to receive and return love. So, God in his sovereign wisdom, provides the perfect solution to sin in the gift of salvation through Jesus Christ. Because we are human beings and not robots, that gift can be received or rejected. It is an individual and a free choice.

Free choice

As I mentioned in an earlier chapter, I prefer the term "free choice" rather than "free will" because neither you nor I could will anything into existence. Yet, often "free will" is the term used in this discussion. Both terms point to the same idea – that humanity has freedom to choose. In fact, God, the Creator and Sovereign Ruler of the universe, has set our lives in motion by giving us freedom to make moral choices. We can choose godly or ungodly. Good or evil.

> *Man's will is free because God is sovereign.*
> *A God less than sovereign could not bestow moral freedom upon His creatures.*
> *He would be afraid to do so.*
>
> **A.W. Tozer**[93]

We have choices and each choice brings consequences. We can choose our thinking, attitudes, and behaviour. We cannot, often, choose the consequences.

> *"Whoever is not with me is against me,*
> *and whoever does not gather with me scatters."*
>
> **Matthew 12:30 ESV**

> *Jesus said to him, "I am the way, and the truth,*
> *and the life. No one comes to the Father*
> *except through me."*
>
> **John 14:6 ESV**

Because of God's amazing mercy and grace, Jesus bore the ultimate consequence of evil on the cross. And because of God's amazing mercy and grace, even after we choose to follow Jesus, we are offered forgiveness every time we sin.

---

[93] A.W. Tozer, *The Knowledge of the Holy*, Harper & Row, 1961, 1975 edition, p. 118.

> *If we confess our sins, he is faithful and just to forgive us our sins and to cleanse us from all unrighteousness.*
> **1 John 1:9 ESV**

So, it comes down to this – humanity's free choice and God's sovereignty are equally true. Think of a long train trip. As with all illustrations, this one will fall short. But it will get us on the right track (pun intended). I'm married to a man who loves trains. We've enjoyed train trips in Europe and we're planning a bucket-list train trip through the heart of this huge continent of Australia, from bottom to top. We are not the creators of the train, we are not the operators of the train. So, we relinquish control and trust in those who have the power.

The entire train trip is sovereignly out of our hands. Yet, we are not left without choices. We can travel southbound or northbound. We can get off in Alice Springs for great adventures in that region. We have free choice when it comes to when we sleep, when we eat, what we eat, with whom we strike up conversations, when we read, when we look out the window. The trip is designed that way.

Imagine what kind of anarchy would ensue if each one who wanted to go on the trip tried to exercise their own complete freedom – changing where tracks went, taking over the operations, removing the tracks completely because they were too constraining… chaos. The existence of the tracks does not reduce our options; it actually allows us to have success with our options. Our freedom of choice and God's sovereignty are not mutually exclusive. In fact, our free choice is part of his sovereign plan.

...God is a loving Creator who has made human beings in his image with a significant capacity to choose, with all its marvelous potential of love, trust, and moral responsibility. God is not the irresistible cause of human behaviour, whether good or bad – otherwise our actions and characters would be deprived of moral significance and it would make no sense to talk of us doing or being "good" or "bad". It is one of God's greatest glories that he invests us with moral significance.
John C. Lennox[94]

Management styles

Did God set the world in motion and then leave it to humans to handle? Or does everything that happens in our day come out of a choice made by God? Or… is it somewhere in between?

I believe in the sovereignty of God. I believe that God is intimately involved in our lives. I believe that God intervenes to stop something dreadful from happening in order to keep us on earth a while longer for some Kingdom purposes. And, yet, I do not believe that God micro-manages. There are examples of this throughout Scripture, both in the Old and New Testaments. Let's take Paul as our example.

When we first meet Paul, in Acts 7:58, he was called Saul; he was present for the stoning of Stephen who is believed to be the first follower of Jesus to be martyred. Chapter 8 of Acts opens with this terse statement, "And Saul approved of their killing him." In the next verses we see that Saul was very involved in the persecution of

---

94 John C. Lennox, *Determined to Believe? The Sovereignty of God, Freedom, Faith, and Human Responsibility*, Lion Hudson, 2017, p. 53.

the early Church. Then our sovereign God directly and dramatically intervened in Saul's life.

Meanwhile, Saul was still breathing out murderous threats against the Lord's disciples. He went to the high priest and asked him for letters to the synagogues in Damascus, so that if he found any there who belonged to the Way, whether men or women, he might take them as prisoners to Jerusalem. As he neared Damascus on his journey, suddenly a light from heaven flashed around him. He fell to the ground and heard a voice say to him, "Saul, Saul, why do you persecute me?"
"Who are you, Lord?" Saul asked.
"I am Jesus, whom you are persecuting," he replied. "Now get up and go into the city, and you will be told what you must do." The men traveling with Saul stood there speechless; they heard the sound but did not see anyone. Saul got up from the ground, but when he opened his eyes he could see nothing. So they led him by the hand into Damascus. For three days he was blind, and did not eat or drink anything.

Acts 9:1-9

From the time of Paul's conversion, onward, did God guide him so directly? No. Indeed, not. Let's look at Paul's own account of what happened. Notice what he says was HIS response. It was not a directive from God.

> *For you have heard of my previous way of life in Judaism, how intensely I persecuted the church of God and tried to destroy it. I was advancing in Judaism beyond many of my own age among my people and was extremely zealous for the traditions of my fathers. But when God, who set me apart from my mother's womb and called me by his grace, was pleased to reveal his Son in me so that I might preach him among the Gentiles, my immediate response was not to consult any human being. I did not go up to Jerusalem to see those who were apostles before I was, but I went into Arabia.*
> *Later I returned to Damascus.*
> **Galatians 1:13-17**

In 2 Timothy 4:9, we read that Paul told Timothy, "Do your best to come to me quickly." And in Acts 20:16, we see that "Paul had decided to sail past Ephesus." Clearly, these are examples of free choice at work.

And then, in contrast, we see the Holy Spirit directly involved in Paul's plans and movements.

> *And they went through the region of Phrygia and Galatia, having been forbidden by the Holy Spirit to speak the word in Asia. And when they had come up to Mysia, they attempted to go into Bithynia, but the Spirit of Jesus did not allow them. So, passing by Mysia, they went down to Troas. And a vision appeared to Paul in the night: a man of Macedonia was standing there, urging him and saying, "Come over to Macedonia and help us." And when Paul had seen the vision, immediately we sought to go on into Macedonia, concluding that God had called us to preach the gospel to them.*
> **Acts 16:6-10 ESV**

Maybe it's a matter of perspective. We make decisions based on what we know, but we don't, often, see the big picture. And we don't, often, see how other pieces fit into that picture. It's like our part in jazz improvisation. Each player has an important role that involves a lot of free choice. Yet there is sovereign structure – maybe an original tune, maybe simply a key signature and time signature. That structure provides the boundaries – what notes are allowed and not allowed at various times, in certain measures or bars. Within that structure, each player has "free rein" so to speak. And, together, they control the results.

Or maybe it could best be described as a dance – our part is to use the mind God gave us, seek direction through prayer and the Word, seek wise counsel, depend on the Holy Spirit to ultimately guide; God's part is to be in ultimate control – to guide, direct, and intervene.

For from him and through him and for him are all things.
To him be the glory forever! Amen.
Romans 11:36

Control issues

Okay, I'll just lay this truth out there. I like to have control of some things in my life – uninterrupted sleep, a perfectly clean home, a place for everything and everything in its place, what I eat and when I eat it… and on and on the list could go. I also like to have control over some other people in my life. I'd like Jim to agree with my point of view on everything, for example.

I'd like everyone to use a napkin/serviette when they eat. While raising our kids, we actually played a game that involved catching a family member without a napkin. The culprit had to apologise to the cook or, if in a restaurant, to the server. We all laugh about the time we were eating in a fast-food restaurant and one kid caught Jim without a napkin on his lap. This was a dilemma because there was no server to whom he could apologise. So, the other four of us determined that his penalty would be that he had to go up to the counter where orders were placed and apologise to the worker, there. What a sight – this fully grown man, stepping into a line of customers and leaning over the counter in order to quietly say, "I'm sorry that I didn't have my napkin on my lap." Though he was trying to avoid being heard by all, he definitely was noticed. And all of the giggles at our table were heard by everyone as well. What a curious group of people we were! Few of my children use napkins as adults so I guess those efforts were all in vain. I've given up trying to control the use of napkins, but I am happy to report that I do have a few grandchildren who have developed a strong appreciation for napkins. I've settled for influence instead of control.

Yet, the most amazing reality of my control issues is that I have control issues with God. When I'm honest with myself, I must admit that there are times when I don't want God to do whatever he wants; I want him to do whatever I want. The problem is that, not only do I want to do things my way, I actually want to MAKE GOD do things my way! Those are some serious control issues, right? I write with a lightness about it but, in truth, there is nothing light-hearted here. It's quite audacious and incredibly foolish to think that I could, or should, control God.

What do my attempts to control God look like? Well, it's when I pray suggestions to God, advising God as to what I think would be a best solution. (Earlier, we talked about Philippians chapter 4 where we are told to present requests, not advice, to God.) It could be when I simply don't pray for something because I don't believe God can do it. I reduce his God-ness. It's also when I do something that I think would make God pleased with me, which would, in my twisted thinking, lead him to give me what I want. I might do something that seems devout or holy in order to impress God. No matter how I do it, the bottom line is that I'm trying to manipulate God in order to get what I want. So. Very. Wrong. So very foolish. I am delighted that God is sovereign and yet... sometimes... I'd rather be the one holding the remote.

So the task is not to get God to do something I think needs to be done, but to become aware of what God is doing so that I can respond to it and participate and take delight in it.

Eugene Peterson[95]

Comfort in the mystery

Our world is from God. Our Bible is from God. Our very life is from God. We try our best to make sense of it all and when we can't fully grasp something, we mustn't simply ignore it or abandon it and live in denial. Nor can we, in order to ease our discomfort, read into Scripture what is not there.

As finite beings, we are forced to this place of admitting that we will never fully grasp the God-ness of our God. I'm reminded of a youth pastor in Alaska I heard, many years ago, say to his students, "If I knew the answer to that, either I'd be as smart as God or he'd be as dumb as me." We can study the Scriptures with great devotion, we can learn from the most gifted theologians, we can read all that there is to read, and still there will be mysteries when it comes to our sovereign God.

Far from increasing human freedom, it is the rejection of God that actually diminishes it and leads to a pseudo-religious anthropocentric ideology, whereby each individual man and woman becomes a prisoner of non-rational forces that will eventually destroy them in complete disregard of their humanity.

John C. Lennox[96]

We are left to believe four things:

- God is.
- He knows what he is doing.
- What he is doing is always good.
- He is fully trustworthy.

---

[96] John C. Lennox, *Determined to Believe? The Sovereignty of God, Freedom, Faith, and Human Responsibility*, Lion Hudson, 2017, p. 34.

Confident trust

God will make a way
Where there seems to be no way
He works in ways we cannot see
He will make a way for me
He will be my guide
Hold me closely to his side
With love and strength for each new day
He will make a way
He will make a way

Don Moen[97]

The above song was our family's theme song during a period of uncertainty. Jim had been transferred from Alaska to Colorado with his company... with four days' notice, I might add. So, the kids and I had to handle all issues relating to wrapping up commitments, making deposits in friendships, squeezing every ounce of love out of every moment with our extended family, reducing things in that category called "Stuff", and all tasks involving relocating. One particular child was really struggling with some anger against God and parents because change was not easy for that one. I can hear Jeri's voice, even now, singing the above chorus over and over... and over some more, as if to comfort and convince the rest of her family that God was sovereign AND fully able. And she can testify that God did, indeed, make a way.

---

[97] *God Will Make A Way*, Don Moen, © 1990 Integrity's Hosanna! Music (Admin. by SHOUT! Music Publishing Australia). Used by permission.

In God's sovereignty, we gain confidence and comfort. Because God is sovereign, we have inner strength and security. Think about this honestly and seriously for a moment: if God's love was limitless (as I believe it is!) yet his control was limited (which I believe it is not!), could you trust him? I think not.

Imagine a really nice doctor, a General Practitioner who is morally upright, incredibly kind, very gentle and comforting... and yet the doctor is not able to help you. General Practitioners are marvellous and serve an important role in medicine, but this doctor has limitations due to lack of specialist training. Will you stay with the nice doctor or will you accept a referral to a specialist? I hope the answer is obvious. We would choose a doctor who is nice and wants to help AND who has the ability to help. The power of their training and their experience, combined with their desire to help, is a potent combination. God is that specialist and so much more! God fully wants to help and is fully able to help. Therefore, we can fully trust him. Hallelujahs abound!

And we know that for those who love God all things work together for good, for those who are called according to his purpose.
Romans 8:28 ESV

We can fully trust that ultimate good will come in every situation as we continue to be a people who love and follow our good, good Father. God's good purposes will come about. We may not see any or all of the good that comes in our lifetime. The truth of God's good purposes does not negate the parallel truth that harmful things are, indeed, harmful. Pain is painful. Evil is evil. Yet, our good, good Father accomplishes good. Sometimes in the middle. Sometimes in the end. The prophet, Jeremiah, never lived to see God's people turn back toward God and live in abundance once more. It happened, though. And we're still talking about Jeremiah's prophecies and God's goodness today.

David praised the Lord in the presence of the whole assembly, saying,
"Praise be to you, Lord,
the God of our father Israel, from everlasting to everlasting.
Yours, Lord, is the greatness and the power
and the glory and the majesty and the splendor,
for everything in heaven and earth is yours.
Yours, Lord, is the kingdom;
you are exalted as head over all.
Wealth and honor come from you;
you are the ruler of all things.
In your hands are strength and power
to exalt and give strength to all.
Now, our God, we give you thanks,
and praise your glorious name."

1 Chronicles 29:10-13

Then I heard what sounded like a great multitude,
like the roar of rushing waters and like loud peals of thunder, shouting:
"Hallelujah! For our Lord God Almighty reigns."

Revelation 19:6

For Reflection

1. Because we cannot fully handle each of the BIG questions this topic raises, here are some of the many resources that may help with further study:

Suffering and Evil:

- C.S. Lewis, ***The Problem of Pain***, The Centenary Press, 1940.
- C.S. Lewis, ***A Grief Observed,*** Faber and Faber, 1961.
- Philip Yancey, ***Where is God When it Hurts?*** Zondervan, 1977.
- Philip Yancey, ***The Question that Never Goes Away: Why?*** Thomas Nelson, 2014.
- Joni Eareckson Tada, ***When God Weeps***, Zondervan, 1997.

Sovereignty:

- John C. Lennox, ***Determined to Believe? The Sovereignty of God, Freedom, Faith, and Human Responsibility,*** Lion Hudson, 2017.

2. Spend some time studying the various names for God. An online search will lead you to them. This is another way to learn more of the character of our God. Challenge a friend to memorise the names of God with you.

3. Control issues. Do you have any? With God? Journal about it and then sit in silence and consider – what is the root reason for those control issues and what steps can you take to avoid further struggles with God? Maybe you have never fully surrendered control of your life to the One who died on the cross for you. Jesus is waiting to be your Saviour and your Lord.

4. Re-read Daniel 3:26. For a moment, consider others around you who do not know Jesus and are worshipping small-g gods. How well does your intimacy with our God and all that he is for YOU cause them to call him the Most High God? Sit with that for a while. Talk with Lord God about it.

15

GOD IS IMMUTABLE

*Then Moses said to God, "If I come to the people of Israel and say to them, 'The God of your fathers has sent me to you,' and they ask me, 'What is his name?' what shall I say to them?" God said to Moses, "**I am who I am**." And he said, "Say this to the people of Israel: '**I am** has sent me to you.'" God also said to Moses, "Say this to the people of Israel: 'The **Lord**, the God of your fathers, the God of Abraham, the God of Isaac, and the God of Jacob, has sent me to you.' This is my name forever, and thus I am to be remembered throughout all generations.*

Exodus 3:13-15 ESV, emphasis added

Many Biblical scholars say that the Hebrew for "I am who I am" is linked to a name for God, which we discussed in the previous chapter – **Yahweh.** It's the name that is written in our Bibles as Lord. Out of reverence for God this word was not spoken and was usually written with only the Hebrew equivalent of these capital letters – **YHWH**. This is how God chose to identify himself to Moses and to the people Moses would be leading. He is I Am. This speaks to both the eternality of God as well as the immutability of God. God is eternal – without beginning and without ending. And God is immutable – always and forever unchanging. Therefore, Jesus Christ, God incarnate – is immutable.

Jesus Christ is the same yesterday and today and forever.
Hebrews 13:8

God is unchanging and constant. God is un-alterable. He cannot be impacted by anything that would, therefore, cause him to change his character in any way. God cannot improve. He cannot grow. He cannot become. Okay, sit with that thought for a bit before you move on.

All that God is He has always been and all that he has been and is he always will be.
Anselm of Canterbury[98]

God is not like us

Again, we are faced with this reality – God is God and we are not. We are mutable. We change our minds and our moods. Quite easily, at times. I have a magnet with this statement, "If it weren't for my mood swings, I wouldn't get any exercise at all." Okay, that's hyperbole and said in jest; however, the reality is that we are fickle people. Perhaps, a bit of Shakespeare via Jane Austen's characters, Marianne Dashwood and Willoughby,[99] is appropriate.

---

[98] Anselm, Archbishop of Canterbury, 1033-1109 AD.
[99] Jane Austen, *Sense and Sensibility*, 1811. Public Domain.

> *Love is not love which alters when its alteration finds,*
> *or bends with the remover to remove: O no! It is an ever-fixed mark*
> *that looks on tempests and is never shaken.*
> **William Shakespeare**[100]

Indeed, in the Jane Austen story, Willoughby professed unchanging love and then that love... well... it changed. It altered in such an extreme way that Marianne suffered immense heartache. Human love, no matter what it professes, is not immutable. In truth, human love can be quite fickle.

Think of what ways you have changed today. Have you changed direction? Changed opinion? Changed goals? Changed moods? Perhaps your dinner plans have changed because someone else changed their mind. Perhaps your plans to hike changed because the weather report changed. Perhaps your entire bathroom renovation plans changed because one contractor changed one aspect of payment that troubled you, ethically. (This is all-too-real. As I write, Jim is now back to square one in the search for someone else to hire.)

But what about

By now, some of you have had this thought – what about the verses that say that God changed his mind? There are a few of such verses, depending upon what translation you are using. So, let's go there. Here's one example.

---

[100] William Shakespeare, Sonnet 116, Public Domain.

> *"I have seen these people,"* the Lord said to Moses, *"and they are a stiff-necked people. Now leave me alone so that my anger may burn against them and that I may destroy them. Then I will make you into a great nation."* But Moses sought the favor of the Lord his God. *"Lord,"* he said, *"why should your anger burn against your people, whom you brought out of Egypt with great power and a mighty hand? Why should the Egyptians say, 'It was with evil intent that he brought them out, to kill them in the mountains and to wipe them off the face of the earth'? Turn from your fierce anger; **relent** and do not bring disaster on your people. Remember your servants Abraham, Isaac and Israel, to whom you swore by your own self: 'I will make your descendants as numerous as the stars in the sky and I will give your descendants all this land I promised them, and it will be their inheritance forever.'"* Then the Lord **relented** and did not bring on his people the disaster he had threatened.
>
> **Exodus 32:9-14, emphasis added**

Once again, I refer you to The Bible Project. They discuss this passage in an episode of a podcast series, appropriately called ***God***[101]. In the story, God is entering into a covenant relationship with his people and, while Moses is up on the mountain solidifying the covenant, God's people build a calf of melted gold. And then they bow before this golden calf, worshipping it and praying to it. Think about this for a moment. This behaviour is comparable to someone committing adultery on their wedding night. It's definitely not all right. So, Moses serves two roles – a voice for God to the people and a mediator between God and the people.

Moses appealed to God's character and affirmed that God is always

---

[101] The Bible Project, https://bibleproject.com/podcast/gods-fusion-humanity-god. Used by permission.

consistent with that very character. The Hebrew word for "relent" involves an emotion that moves one to feel differently. From our limited perspective, we might see it as though God had changed his mind. In fact, some translations, in place of "relent", do say "change his mind". It would seem more appropriate, however, to say that God had a change of heart, not a change of mind. Though he was angry and saddened by the so-soon broken covenant, he would relent and be patient with his people. Thus, when speaking to God, Moses was actually appealing to God's consistency. He was asking the God who never changes to never change. No matter how God is feeling about his people, he never breaks a covenant. He is a covenant-keeping God.

This is just one example, of many, in which God's justice meets God's love (plus a whole lot of other attributes). Justice, on its own, would say, "That's enough!" Yet a complete picture of justice would say that, within a covenant, justice requires grace. It requires an opportunity for his people to repent. And in this golden calf example we see God's sovereignty interacting with human freedom. God chooses to work with, and through, humanity. So, God "relents".

Let's bring this difficult concept home, so to speak, to our son, Brad – a brilliant thinker, a creative, someone who thinks outside the box. There was a season when he was young, a very long season, in which I felt that he should become an attorney. He was very good at building a case. He presented many-a valid argument in order for us, as his parents, to "change our minds". Sometimes his argument was so solid that we had to, as flawed parents, change our minds. Sometimes we quietly agreed, Jim and I, that his argument was a smashing success but we couldn't, this time, change our minds.

And sometimes, we actually created the chance for him to present his case. His thought processes were excellent and I enjoyed seeing his mind at work. In some of those situations, from his perspective, we changed our minds. From our perspective, we had given him an opportunity to do what we wanted him to do all along. You know – Parenting 101: every idea seems brilliant to a child if it comes from them. Could it be that God works that way with us, sometimes? Of course, he's the perfect parent and has wisdom far beyond any earthling. But maybe that is some of what we see in the Old Testament examples where God relents. And some of the other instances fall into that category called "Mystery", which we have discussed before!

Hope

I have this hope
As an anchor for my soul
Through every storm
I will hold to You
With endless love
All my fear is swept away
In everything
I will trust in You

There is hope in the promise of the cross
You gave everything to save the world You love

And this hope is an anchor for my soul
Our God will stand unshakable

Unchanging One
You who was and is to come
Your promise sure
You will not let go[102]

We've looked at some of these lyrics earlier. This time, I want to focus on one aspect – the hope we have because of our soul's anchor. Because God will never change who he is, his children have great hope. We never have to fear a change of mind nor a change of mood. God is who he is. We can rest. We can rest in peace, in security, in safety. We can rest with hope. That hope is an anchor. It is an anchor deep in our gut; it is an anchor for our souls.

Therefore, brothers and sisters, since we have confidence to enter the Most Holy Place by the blood of Jesus, by a new and living way opened for us through the curtain, that is, his body, and since we have a great priest over the house of God, let us draw near to God with a sincere heart and with the full assurance that faith brings, having our hearts sprinkled to cleanse us from a guilty conscience and having our bodies washed with pure water. **Let us hold unswervingly to the hope we profess, for he who promised is faithful.** *And let us consider how we may spur one another on toward love and good deeds, not giving up meeting together, as some are in the habit of doing, but encouraging one another— and all the more as you see the Day approaching.*
Hebrews 10:19-25, emphasis added

This is truly an amazing hope. The immutable God invites us to draw near to him. Because he is unchanging, we know that we are able to draw near to him with complete trust, with "the full assurance that faith brings", as it says, above. And then consider, for a moment, how this hope affects our "one anothers". Our relationships with each other, when anchored in our unchanging God, have great hope. We can draw near to God AND we can draw near to one another. We can spur one another on, we can be faithful in meeting together, and we can encourage one another because of the new and living way that was opened for us through the curtain.

And there is at least one more way that we have great hope in the context of God's immutability. It's a big deal, actually. Here is our reality – we. are. not. immutable. You are very mutable. I am very mutable; in that I find great hope. This is absolutely fantastic news! Follow me, here. Because you and I are NOT immutable, you and I are not stuck. We are not stuck in our sinfulness and we are not stuck in our sickness. We have hope that we can grow. If we seem stuck, we still can be un-stuck. We can be changed because of the One who cannot be changed. Let that thought sink in.

And we all, who with unveiled faces contemplate the Lord's glory,
*are being **transformed** into his image with ever-increasing glory,*
which comes from the Lord, who is the Spirit.
2 Corinthians 3:18, emphasis added

For Reflection

1. For further study, check out **Deuteronomy (Understanding the Bible Commentary Series)**.[103]

2. Listen to the full podcast referenced in this chapter – The Bible Project's **God Series**, Episode 7.[104] There's a lot to consider in that one podcast, alone! (And there are more terrific podcasts in the series.)

3. Re-read Hebrews 10:19-25. Consider the hope that you profess. Write about it. Explain it to a friend. This will help you hold unswervingly to it.

4. Ponder the truth that we have great hope BECAUSE we are mutable. We actually can grow. We can become more like Jesus. Think of things about yourself that you would like to change, some things where you seem a bit stuck. Talk with God about those desires right now. Thank God for the Holy Spirit who is within you. Invite him to do his transformative work.

---

[103] Christopher J. H. Wright, Deuteronomy, Understanding the Bible Commentary Series, Baker Books, 2012.
[104] The Bible Project, https://bibleproject.com/podcast/gods-fusion-humanity-god. Used by permission.

CONCLUDING THOUGHTS

Becoming what we behold

Our daughter, Jeri, had a cat that she called Emma the Prairie Kitten. Emma was born to a barn cat belonging to friends who lived out on the edge of civilisation in Colorado. It was where houses on large acreage opened onto untouched prairies. Those prairies were home to thousands of adorable creatures that many felt were not very adorable after all – prairie dogs. (They've been known to be pests, but can we blame them for following their instincts when their burrows are destroyed for new construction?!) When she was relaxed, Emma would often sit like a prairie dog – upright, with all body weight resting on her tail and hind legs, with her front paws held up near her chin in almost a praying position. You can see the reason for her nickname. We truly believe that Emma's first sighting, after birth, was a prairie dog. And she mimicked what she first saw. She became what she beheld.

We, too, become what we behold. We are being transformed by the things on which we focus. This thought bears repeating from the previous chapter. Here is a verse we've recently read, this time in a different translation.

And we all, with unveiled face, beholding the glory of the Lord, are being transformed into the same image from one degree of glory to another. For this comes from the Lord who is the Spirit.
2 Corinthians 3:18 ESV

We need to fix what we fix our eyes on. Too often our eyes are fixed on the problems around us, the things we don't have, the people who irritate us. In order to become more and more like Christ, we need to fix our eyes on him. Do your eyes need fixing?

Character clusters

Maybe this will help. Think in terms of character clusters, groupings of attributes of God that work together in your situation. For instance, when I'm praying for someone that I love, who is in what looks like a desperate situation, I think of this cluster – God's love, wisdom, and power. God loves them more than I ever could. He knows what is the absolutely BEST outcome for their situation. And he has the complete power to accomplish what he knows is best. That fixes my thinking as I fix my focus on the truth of who God is.

God's justice, righteousness, and mercy – that cluster impacts the way I view social prejudices and it impacts the way I interact with people and ideas around such issues. Fixing my focus on God fixes the way I view others.

God's patience, grace and compassion – that cluster helps me as I meet a person who is, by all appearances, an adult but is, emotionally, quite stunted in their growth. Instead of judging them, I can offer God's patience, grace and compassion, which is at work in me and through me. My heart is fixed as I fix my heart on him.

I encourage you to think of God's character throughout your day. As you encounter various bumps and dilemmas, think of the cluster of attributes that best relates to your situation. In truth, we are unbelievably blessed. We just need to see it.

> *With the goodness of God to desire our highest welfare,*
> *the wisdom of God to plan it, and the power of God*
> *to achieve it, what do we lack?*
> *Surely we are the most favored of all creatures.*
> **A.W. Tozer**[105]

Knowing

> *I want to know Christ—yes, to know the power of his resurrection*
> *and participation in his sufferings, becoming like him in his death, and so,*
> *somehow, attaining to the resurrection from the dead.*
> **Philippians 3:10-11**

When I was very young, I memorised this passage in the Amplified paraphrase. The writers chose to explain the words "to know Christ" this way – "that I may progressively become more deeply and intimately acquainted with Him, perceiving and recognizing and understanding the wonders of His Person more strongly and more clearly" (AMPCE). To this day, those word choices resonate with me – progressively, more deeply, intimately, perceiving, recognising, understanding. And certainly "the wonders of His Person" is

---
[105] A.W. Tozer, *The Knowledge of the Holy*, Harper & Row, 1961, 1975 edition, p. 70.

such a beautiful way to describe the character of God. Who he is... is, indeed, a wonder.

This word "know" in the Greek is part of a word cluster around the noun ***gnosis.*** I'll never forget the day I was studying another passage of scripture in the New Testament and I first ran across that word cluster in Greek. I called my pastor to verify that, from my limited grasp of Greek, I was getting it right. It was a huge breakthrough in my understanding of understanding God! I was in that marvellous prayer in the middle of the book of Ephesians.

---

*For this reason I bow my knees before the Father, from whom every family in heaven and on earth is named, that according to the riches of his glory he may grant you to be strengthened with power through his Spirit in your inner being, so that Christ may dwell in your hearts through faith—that you, being rooted and grounded in love, may have strength to comprehend with all the saints what is the breadth and length and height and depth, and to **<u>know</u>** the love of Christ that surpasses **<u>knowledge</u>**, that you may be filled with all the fullness of God. Now to him who is able to do far more abundantly than all that we ask or think, according to the power at work within us, to him be glory in the church and in Christ Jesus throughout all generations, forever and ever. Amen.*

Ephesians 3:14-21 ESV, emphasis added

Prior to that day, I had always thought that Paul was praying this way - that you would experientially and intimately know the love of God which surpasses intellectual knowledge. And that had made sense to me. Heart knowledge over head knowledge. We could learn so many amazing facts about God's character and yet knowing God intimately and personally surpasses head knowledge every time. Right? You're with me on that one? We don't want to just settle for intellectual understanding. We want intimacy.

However **ginosko, gnosis, gnonai,** ... all of the Greek words in this word cluster refer to intimate knowledge. The words are about recognising, perceiving, coming to know, growing in understanding. These words are, appropriately, used in reference to sexual intimacy.

So the verse actually reads - that you would intimately know the love of Christ which surpasses all that you could ever intimately know. Amazing! This is the beyond of God - that his love for you is far beyond whatever you could experientially and intimately know. Ever. As you grow in your relationship with God, he always knows that there is more. There is more love and there is more understanding of that love. The intimate love of God for you - the more you know, the more you know you don't know.

A question for each of us

Where do we each go from here?

Well, my first answer is – nowhere.

Absolutely nowhere. I need to gaze at my God for all time. He must be my focus. You need to be focused on him, too. We need to be getting to know him more and more each day. We need it quite desperately, actually.

And my second answer is – everywhere.

Consider our world that desperately needs God. Imagine what a difference could be made if that world, without counterfeits and distractions, only saw one God – the God who lives in you and me.

Nowhere and everywhere

How do we go nowhere and everywhere at the same time? It involves knees and it involves walking. It's about God's presence and my dependence. I want to walk through the rest of my life on my knees. Of course, this is metaphorical, but does it make sense? It's an image that I try to carry with me each day. If my attitude is one of dependence upon God in prayer, if my attitude is one of being in his presence at all times, if I am aware that he is very present, then I am more apt to stop trying to be my own god.

Imagine an entire company of Christians, a whole band of believers, all walking through their days on their knees. Imagine all of us, in every sphere of life, living in complete surrender to and living in total dependence on our Creator, our Redeemer, our Lord. We become what we behold. Let's be a people who continually behold our God – that we may know him, personally and increasingly, and that the world around us would come to know him, personally and increasingly. Are you with me?

If you declare with your mouth, "Jesus is Lord," and believe in your heart that God raised him from the dead, you will be saved. For it is with your heart that you believe and are justified, and it is with your mouth that you profess your faith and are saved.

Romans 10:9-10

Perhaps while reading this book, you have realised that you do not have a personal relationship with God at all. Maybe you believe he exists and you know a lot about him, but you don't know him, personally. That's really what our whole existence on earth is about and that's why Jesus was born into humanity. The death and resurrection of Jesus is the pivotal point of history, but maybe you have not let Jesus personally pivot your history. Please don't close this book without asking Jesus to become your personal Saviour.

You have free choice and God has been very patiently waiting for you to choose him. There is no magic formula for becoming a follower of Jesus. It just involves a decision and a declaration. If you are struggling with what to say to God about wanting to follow him, here is a simple prayer that you could use. There is no special way to pray it; sometimes we close our eyes in order to concentrate more fully on what we're praying but that would make reading the prayer impossible! Speaking out loud is helpful as it seems more like a serious declaration but even that is not necessary because God hears your heart. The important thing is that you take the step, pivoting FROM how you've been living your life in your own efforts and turning TOWARD Jesus and following him from now on.

Dear God,

I admit that I need you. I'm done living my life on my own and avoiding you. I know that I have sinned and I ask you, now, to forgive me for all of my sin. Thank you, Jesus, that you paid the penalty for my sin when you died on the cross. I want to make a new start right now, with great hope for my future. I want to be a Christian, a follower of Jesus Christ, for the rest of my life, every single day. Thank you for your mercy and grace in forgiving me and giving me everlasting life.

In Jesus' name, amen!

GRATITUDE

The first person I must thank is Darin Markwardt. Remember, back in the day, when you were a ten-year-old in K-5 Church in Palmer, Alaska and you lead a little "band of brothers" in the writing of The Attribute Rap as a review of our unit on the character of God? I had no idea that it would be my permanent go-to when thinking through a list on the attributes of God. Thank you for creating something that has stuck with so many of us for so long!

I am incredibly grateful for the editorial expertise and the project management skills of Celina Mina. Your brilliant insight is exactly what I needed. Thank you, Stuart Smith, for your amazing book design and layout work. I am immensely grateful for your diligence. To Josh Olson, Brianna Wheeler and Bec O'Brien – thank you for your wisdom and guidance in processes that were totally new to me.

Thank you to everyone who was eager and willing to read a full manuscript draft – Michael Godfrey, Ebony Hindle, Elizabeth Lamb, Elise Heerde. Your feedback and perspectives are highly valued contributions. And thank you to the many in our church family who checked in on my progress and supported me in prayer.

Each of you in the Connect Group that I lead have been so encouraging. Our discussions around the character of God were one of the factors that prompted me to begin writing. Hugs to Uthra, Jemima, Rachel, Olivia, Bianca, and our newest member - Megan.

Finally, I have huge gratitude to my family here in Australia – Jim, Jeri, Brad and Karissa, Joey and Meyling. Thank you for your belief in this project. Your input and encouragement are treasured. Jim, thank you for letting this be my focus for this season. I'm so glad that I let you join me on that writing retreat when you said, "If I promise not to talk, could I be there, too?" Jeri, your proofreading and editing skills are a life-saving gift for which my thanks is only surpassed by my gratitude for our friendship.

ABOUT THE AUTHOR

Sharon and her husband, Jim, began to consider making Australia their home when their first grandchild was born in Australia. With many roots deeply set in Alaska, USA, the whole family is now happily settled in Queensland. Jim and Sharon's kids, spouses, and eight grandchildren live within 50 minutes of each other – quite stunning for a family who never expected to leave Alaska.

Sharon has worn many hats over the years – teacher, ministry director, pastor, mentor... in various church and para-church ministries in Alaska and Colorado, both as a volunteer and as part of the pastoral team. She has also been a primary school teacher, a music teacher, an English as a Second Language teacher, and a co-worker with Jim in corporate offices for a season.

When they became empty-nesters, Jim and Sharon put their household in storage as Sharon followed Jim in his career opportunities with the company for which he worked for more than 36 years. That adventure took them to Nigeria, Indonesia, and Saudi Arabia. Sharon is forever grateful for that decade full of change, which reshaped her thinking about God and this humanity-packed planet, deepening her commitment to the Gospel of Jesus Christ and deepening her love of God. Jim and Sharon are a part of the team and family at Hillsong Church Gold Coast, Queensland, Australia.